GOD OF THE UNEXPECTED

By the same author:

The Pilgrim God: A Biblical Journey
(Washington: The Pastoral Press, 1985/Dublin:
Veritas, 1990)

*The Way of the Lord: A New Testament
Pilgrimage*
(The Pastoral Press/Veritas, 1990)

Praying the Our Father Today
(The Pastoral Press, 1992)

GOD OF THE UNEXPECTED

Newness and the Spirit in the Bible

BROTHER JOHN OF TAIZÉ

GEOFFREY
CHAPMAN
MOWBRAY

Geoffrey Chapman Mowbray
A Cassell imprint
Wellington House
125 Strand
London
WC2R 0BB

215 Park Avenue South
New York
NY 10003

First published 1995

A French edition of this book was published in 1994 in
collaboration with Brepols: *La Nouveauté et l'Esprit:
Introductions bibliques*, © Ateliers et Presses de Taizé, F71250,
1994.

British Library Cataloguing in Publication Data.
A catalogue record for this book is available from the British
Library.

ISBN 0-264-67403-0

Printed and bound in Great Britain by Cox & Wyman Ltd,
Reading

CONTENTS

INTRODUCTION

For a quarter of a century now, tens of thousands of young adults in their twenties have been finding their way to the village of Taizé in Burgundy, France. They go to take part in week-long gatherings of prayer and sharing around the brothers of the ecumenical Christian community founded during World War II in that village by Brother Roger. The Taizé Community has constantly looked for ways to help those who come there, from Eastern and Western Europe as well as from other continents, to discover the sources of faith in Christ, one of the most important of which is an understanding of the Bible.

Each morning, therefore, visitors to Taizé listen to a brother give a Bible introduction, a short talk which is translated simultaneously into several different languages. They then divide into small groups to reflect on passages of Scripture, using questions which apply the texts to their daily existence. This book is based on two related series of these introductions: one centred on the Holy Spirit, the other on the theme of 'newness' in the Bible.

In a world of constant change, biblical faith can appear out-of-date, irrelevant to the concerns of contemporary life. And yet the Bible brings us into contact with a God whose hallmark is the ability to do something new (Isa 43.19). Encountering this God means being pulled out of stifling or comfortable routines and seeing unexpected new horizons open before our eyes. We discover faith as an adventure, a journey in God's company along a road full of surprises, a call to live a life beyond all our dreams.

These reflections shed new light on the biblical theme of creation. They likewise deepen our understanding of the figure of the Holy Spirit, God's creative breath that sets us on the road to reconciliation.

The questions given at the end of each short chapter can be used for personal reflection, or adapted to the needs of a church or school discussion group.

The Spirit came down upon the Son of God become Son of Man, accustoming himself with him to dwell in the human race, to rest upon human beings, ... accomplishing in them the Father's will and renewing them by bringing them from their oldness to the Newness of Christ. (...) What new reality did the Lord bring by his coming? Well, know that he brought all newness in bringing his own self announced in advance, for what was announced ahead of time was precisely this: that Newness would come to renew and reanimate man.

St Irenaeus of Lyons

The Spirit of the Lord, who animates man renewed in Christ, continually breaks down the horizons within which his understanding likes to find security and the limits to which his activity would willingly restrict itself; there dwells within him a power which urges him to go beyond every system and every ideology.

Paul VI

PART ONE

BEAUTY ANCIENT AND FOREVER NEW

St Augustine

I

BRINGER OF THE NEW

THE GOSPEL OF MARK tells us that one Sabbath day, at the beginning of his public ministry, Jesus entered the synagogue in the town of Capernaum and began to teach those who were gathered there (Mark 1.21–28). As a pious Jew, the carpenter from Nazareth was faithful to the custom of his people, who would meet regularly in a simple room or house to listen to the reading of the Scriptures and to receive instruction.

But all of a sudden, in the midst of this thoroughly traditional scene, something unexpected happens: 'And they were astonished at his teaching, for he was teaching them like someone who had authority ... And they were all so astounded that they asked one another, "What is this? A new teaching, given with authority!"' (Mark 1.22, 27). Something different, something unheard of breaks into the everyday routines of the inhabitants of Capernaum, thus provoking a reaction of astonishment. Here we have a first sign, still fragile and even somewhat ambiguous, that bears witness to the presence of God: Jesus is the bearer of a newness that astounds.

At the same time, in the word used twice by Mark to characterize Jesus' teaching, we receive an important clarification. Jesus teaches *with authority*. Far from being just 'empty words', the speech of Jesus is effective; it is able to disperse the forces of evil and restore the fullness of life to an afflicted man. The word 'authority' also emphasizes the fact that the new reality that becomes present through Jesus is not some sort of arbitrary innovation. Jesus' teaching is not 'new' in the sense that it marks a break with what is contained in the sacred books of Israel or is based on brand-new foundations. If the hearers are astonished and have the impression of discovering something as if for the very first time, that is because Jesus is capable of giving life to words that have come down through the ages; he restores their freshness by making them express what they always wanted to say. He removes the layers of ashes that were hiding the glowing coal or, to change the image, he breaks the ice and lets the fountain gush forth once again.

This image of something new that breaks into the normal course of world events can be seen as the 'signature' of the God of the Bible. At the opposite extreme from a sovereign comfortably seated on a faraway throne, God ceaselessly comes to meet human beings in order to open up unexpected horizons for them. Encountering this God means being uprooted from the routines of a world doomed to die in order to participate in the dynamism of an origin that gives life and that makes new.

In the following chapters, we shall use the notion of newness as a key to unlock the meaning of the Bible's message. At the same time, while it sheds light on different aspects of this message, the very notion of newness will become more precise in the course of our investigation. It will be seen to be more and more clearly distinct from all the other meanings given by our world to the word 'new'.

For example, in order to function properly, a so-called consumer society must constantly place new products on the market. Such a society employs a significant amount of energy to convince its members, through tried-and-tested advertising techniques, that buying the latest of these products is essential for health, happiness and fulfilment. But upon reflection, it is obvious that practically nothing distinguishes in quality the most recent of these goods from those of the past month or the past year. This year's ski jacket and toothpaste are new simply because they are the latest in a long line, doomed before too long to become out-of-date in their turn. But God's newness is not of this sort. It has nothing to do with running after the latest fashion.

Let us take another example. One of the characteristics of contemporary Western civilization, increasingly referred to as a 'post-modern society', is a certain *banalization* of the new. In a traditional society, what matters most is the way of organizing life handed down from past generations; anything new is viewed with disdain and suspicion. The shift to modernity radically transforms this way of looking at things. In a modern society, the new is attractive by its very nature. It is seen as the most recent example of a continuous and inevitable progress.

Today, as a result of both the accelerating rate of change and the shipwreck of dreams of an imminent golden age, the new is tending to lose its favourable connotations. It is becoming simply a fact of contemporary life, neither more nor less. At the risk of sounding paradoxical, one can say that change is no longer the bearer of newness: the new, domesticated, ceases to have an impact. One more reason to rediscover, by investigating the Judaeo-Christian Scriptures, something new that stays new, that brings us perpetually into contact with the origin — in short, the newness of a Source.

Questions for Reflection

1. Have I had experiences in my own life like that of those who listened to Jesus, of something new that astonishes and helps to grasp something of the living God? When and how?
2. Where, in my own life and in society, do I sense the need for a new beginning?
3. What aspects of the life and teaching of Jesus found in the gospels still seem new to me?

II

A STORY OF LIBERATION

THE GOSPELS show us Jesus preaching in the synagogues of his people, where people gathered (and where Jewish believers still gather) to read and reflect on the Scriptures. These Scriptures were obviously not identical to our Bible but, rather, included the books found in the first part of the Christian Bible, the 'Old Testament'.* To refer to their Scriptures, the Jewish tradition employs the expression 'the Law and the Prophets' (e.g. Matt 7.12; Luke 16.16; Acts 13.15; Rom 3.21) or more comprehensively 'the Law, the Prophets and the (other) Writings' (cf. Luke 24.44). The expression 'the Law', incidentally, is a rather unfortunate translation of the Hebrew word *Torah*, which literally means 'teaching' and which refers in this context to the first five books of the Bible, the 'books of Moses' which form the heart of the Hebrew Bible. Far from

---

*The expression 'testament' is an inexact translation, by way of Greek and Latin, of the Hebrew word *berith*, which means first of all 'covenant'. Since God's gifts are irrevocable (Rom 11.29), it would be preferable to speak of the 'first Covenant' or, better yet, simply of the 'Book of the Covenant'. One of the principal themes of this book will be to show that God's newness does not abolish the old but renews or transfigures it (cf. Matt 5.17–18).

being merely a list of laws, these books tell above all the story of the origins of the people of God.

Every people, in fact, needs to discover its place in the world, often through telling stories, in order to understand its identity. For the people of Israel, the foundational narratives are found in the Torah and in the other biblical books. But someone who attempts to read these books today can be put off by the difficulty and the diversity of their content. It is a world quite different from our own, and this makes it hard to understand events and their meaning. In particular, we are unsure how to distinguish what is truly important from what is secondary — is there a core of belief, a centre around which everything else can find its appropriate place? Can we discover anything like a basic confession of faith, something similar to our Apostles' Creed?

It seems that we can. Scholars have identified in the Hebrew Scriptures fragments of creeds or confessions of faith. The same thing, incidentally, is true of the New Testament: if we are never given a full and explicit confession of faith, we should not jump to the conclusion that such texts only came into being at a later date. The books of the Bible are not a systematic course of catechesis or theology; they do not claim to be exhaustive.

One of these expressions of the 'creed' of Israel is found in the fifth book of Moses, known as Deuteronomy. At harvest time, the farmer would offer the first-fruits to God as a gesture of thanksgiving. He did this by bringing them to a place of worship, where they were offered symbolically to God by a priest. When the farmer handed over his gifts to the priest, he spoke the following words:

A wandering Aramean was my ancestor; he went down into Egypt and lived there as an alien, few in number, and there he became a great nation, mighty and populous. When the Egyptians treated us harshly and afflicted us, by imposing hard labour on us, we cried to the Lord, the God of our ancestors; the Lord heard our voice and saw our affliction, our toil, and our oppression. The Lord brought us out of Egypt with a mighty hand and an outstretched arm, with a terrifying display of power, and with signs and wonders; and he brought us into this place and gave us this land, a land flowing with milk and honey. So now I bring the first of the fruit of the ground that you, O Lord, have given me.

(Deut 26.5–10)

This text sums up the essential lines of the story told in the whole Torah. It is a tale of *liberation*: God comes to human beings reduced to slavery in order to offer them a new life, a life of freedom, made concrete in the gift of a land: 'The Lord saw our affliction ... brought us out of Egypt ... and brought us into this place.' For the people of Israel, the Exodus from Egypt represents the heart of their faith, the touchstone that enables them to understand the identity of their God and, indirectly, their own identity as God's people.

And here, right at the start, we encounter the theme of newness. Biblical faith is not based on ahistorical myths but on a God who reveals himself by coming into the world to do something new. Very early in its history, Israel was aware of this unique character of its faith:

For ask now about former ages, long before your own, ever since the day that God created human beings on the earth; ask from one end of heaven to the other: has anything so great as this ever happened or has its like ever been heard of? Has any people ever heard the voice of a god speaking out of a fire, as you have heard, and lived? Or has any god ever attempted to go and take a nation for himself from the midst of another nation, by trials, by signs and wonders, by war, by a mighty hand and an outstretched arm, and by terrifying displays of power, as the Lord your God did for you in Egypt before your very eyes?

(Deut 4.32–34)

This awareness of being a people unlike any other (cf. Num 23.9) was so strong in Israel that the people of the Bible ran the risk of viewing it as a privilege or as something they deserved. For this reason, the nation's spiritual leaders had constantly to remind them that their liberation was a pure gift of divine goodness:

It was not because you were more numerous than any other people that the Lord set his heart on you and chose you — for you were the fewest of all peoples. It was because the Lord loved you and kept the oath that he swore to your ancestors, that the Lord has brought you out with a mighty hand, and redeemed you from the house of slavery, from the hand of Pharaoh king of Egypt.

(Deut 7.7–8)

In these ancient texts, the explosion of newness in the world caused by God's coming is expressed by phrases such as 'signs and wonders', 'a mighty hand and an outstretched arm', 'terrifying displays of power', and so on. Such images cause great difficulty for people today who wish to deepen their understanding of the Bible: in those far-off days, the presence of God was often linked to images of war, to the experience of victory in battle. So where, we ask, is the God of love? Must we carefully distinguish the God of the Old Testament, fierce and bloodthirsty, from the God of Jesus Christ, overflowing with love and kindness?

From the beginning of the Christian era, there have been attempts to resolve the dilemma by saying that the Old Testament God is different. Unfortunately, such attempts lead only to a caricature of both the faith of Israel and the message of Jesus Christ. The true path to a solution lies elsewhere, first of all by realizing that the God of the Bible is revealed in and through realities of the world without being confused with them. Like a good educator, God speaks to the human beings of every age in a language they can understand, to lead them to a deeper understanding of his loving designs.

In the second place, it is important to understand more precisely in what sense the 'signs and wonders' caused by 'the outstretched arm' of God are an expression of the divine presence. In this respect, we possess a more complete and more encompassing outlook than the contemporaries of these events. We are able to understand that, in these narratives, what matters is not the fact that a god wages war on behalf of his clients and defeats their enemies — a more or less common way of thinking at the time — but the overturning of the law that 'might makes right'.

Even a cursory glance at human history shows us that, in all times and places, the powerful and the unscrupulous tend to dominate the weak and the poor. Here, perhaps for the first time in human history, this seemingly inexorable law is countermanded by a 'stronger' hand (cf. Luke 11.20–22). The new situation brought about by God's entry into human history is one of ensuring that violence and oppression do not have the last word: justice is revealed as a more fundamental reality.

The essential characteristics of God's coming in the Exodus story are recapitulated in the event recounted in chapters 14 and 15 of the book of Exodus. After having left the land of Egypt, the Israelites make camp on the shores of the sea, where the Egyptians catch up with them. They are quite literally in a dead-end situation, with the enemy at their back and the water in front. And it is precisely in that situation — and nowhere else — that God becomes present and reveals his identity.

Starting from the version of the text that has come down to us, we cannot reconstruct with scientific precision exactly what happened. But the significance of the event is clear: in this impasse, humanly speaking, God opened a road to freedom, a road towards the future. It is not surprising that, in Israel, this event was celebrated in worship as the archetypical intervention of God (cf. Pss 66.6; 77.19; 106.9ff.; 114.3). In it, God's identity shines forth clearly. God's 'signs and wonders' are, in the final analysis, acts that open up a way for human beings imprisoned in a situation without hope of escape.

But if the God of the Exodus is fundamentally the bringer of the new and unexpected, the story underlines as well the dimension of historical continuity. The God who listens to the cry of the poor and who comes to save them is 'the God of your ancestors', 'the God of Abraham, the God of Isaac and the God of Jacob' (Exod 3.15), who acts 'to keep the oath that he swore to your ancestors' (Deut 7.8), to be faithful to his promises. Once again we see that, in the Bible, newness and continuity with the past are not mutually exclusive. The God who does something new is the same one who is always present for his people, constantly ready to break their chains once again.

Questions for Reflection

1. The following texts describe God's entry into our human world: Genesis 12.1–4; 18.1–14; 21.9–21; 1 Kings 17.7–16. What are the consequences of this? What is the new thing that God brings?
2. In the Bible, God's newness is revealed in exemplary fashion by allowing human beings to escape from a hopeless situation, by breaking the material and spiritual chains that kept them captive. Have I had such experiences of liberation in my life? From what? How?

III

·❀·

IN SEARCH OF A RESPONSE

AT THE HEART of the Hebrew Scriptures, we witness the newness of God breaking into the world: in the event of the Exodus, a people draws its existence not from its own strength or its human qualities but from the creative activity of God. The very existence of this people thus reveals the identity of the Source of its life.

This becomes explicit when Moses and the Israelites arrive at Mount Sinai (Exod 19). There, God makes a covenant with the liberated slaves, considering them, in other words, as '[his] treasured possession out of all the peoples' (Exod 19.5) and thus turning an assorted group of individuals and families into a people, a historical subject. According to the Bible, unlike all the other nations on the face of the earth, there is thus one whose existence flows directly from its relationship with God. In the language of Scripture, the covenant with God makes Israel into 'a priestly kingdom and a holy nation' (Exod 19.6). In the ancient world, a priest was an intermediary between a divinity and human beings; Israel's role is therefore to communicate, by its existence, the identity and the will of the living God to the whole of humanity. The unseen God becomes manifest in the world by his shadow, so to speak, by the people that bears his Name.

In consequence, this gift of a covenant is at the same time a great responsibility. The people are called to 'obey [God's] voice and keep [God's] covenant' (Exod 19.5). Although God always takes the initiative in this relationship, human beings are not simply beneficiaries, or passive spectators: their response to God's activity becomes an essential part of that activity. Human beings, created in the image of God (cf. Gen 1.27), are not robots; they are called to cor-respond to God's creativity, in other words to respond to God's call.

This response to God who comes into the life of human beings to do something new can take a variety of forms. We have already seen some of them. The astonishment of Jesus' hearers (Mark 1.22, 27) is a first sign that the newness of God has burst into their lives. The crossing of the sea during the Exodus provides us with a more developed response: the prophetess Miriam sings a hymn of thanksgiving (Exod 15). Here, mere wonder is transformed into gratitude, into praise for what God is and for what God has done.

It is in this context that we can grasp the true meaning of the Law, in the more restricted meaning of the term. In the logic of the Bible, the commandments are above all a response to the new thing God has done. This becomes clear in the following text where, in response to the child's question, the 'creed' telling of God's deeds is clearly indicated as the basic motive for the people's way of life:

When your children ask you in time to come, 'What is the meaning of the decrees and the statutes and the ordinances that the Lord our God has commanded you?' then you shall say to your children, 'We were Pharaoh's slaves in Egypt, but the Lord brought us out of Egypt with a mighty hand. The Lord displayed before our eyes great and awesome signs and wonders against Egypt, against Pharaoh and all his household. He brought us out from there in order to bring us in, to give us the land that he promised on oath to our ancestors. Then the Lord commanded us to observe all these statutes, to fear the Lord our God, for our lasting good, so as to keep us alive, as is now the case. If we diligently observe this entire commandment before the Lord our God, as he has commanded us, we will be in the right.'

(Deut 6.20–25)

The Law is thus not viewed as a starting point to create a relationship with God, a means of pleasing God in order to ensure favourable treatment. It is rather the *consequence* of a relationship instituted by God through an act of liberation, a way for human beings to keep alive that relationship by walking in the Lord's footsteps (cf. Deut 5.32–33). The Bible tells us that the very existence of a people born of the creative act of the God who comes into the world to do something new is a revelation of the identity and the presence of this God. For that reason, it is essential that the day-to-day life of the people correspond to the truth of its origins and its being. But since we are dealing with human beings capable of making choices, this cannot be automatic. God cannot force or manipulate and still be true to himself: instead, the God of the Bible *calls* human beings to follow his ways.

Here we are at the opposite extreme from a legalistic, guilt-ridden attitude, so often — both in the past and in the present — attributed wrongly to the Jewish people. The divine commandments are above all an attempt to allow the newness of God to penetrate the concrete, historical life of a people, so that this newness may find a home on this earth. They are a call to make use of memory and intelligence so that a new way of living may spring up among human beings:

The alien who resides with you shall be to you as the citizen among you; you shall love the alien as yourself, for you were aliens in the land of Egypt: I am the Lord your God.

(Lev 19.34; cf. Exod 23.1–9)

Questions for Reflection

1. When Jesus sums up all the precepts in the double commandment of love (Mark 12.28–34), has he correctly understood the meaning of the Torah? Why does he say that he has not come to abolish the Law and the Prophets but to fulfil them (Matt 5.17)?
2. Concretely, by what way of life can we express our gratitude for God's mercy towards us?

IV

A DEMANDING TRUST

ABOVE AND beyond the Exodus event, the story of a God who breaks into the life of human beings to do something unheard of and to provoke a response goes back to the very beginnings of God's people. It can already be found in the call of Abraham, in chapter 12 of the book of Genesis:

Now the Lord said to Abram, 'Go from your country and your kindred and your father's house to the land that I will show you. I will make of you a great nation, and I will bless you, and make your name great, so that you will be a blessing. I will bless those who bless you, and the one who curses you I will curse; and in you all the families of the earth shall be blessed.'

(Gen 12.1–3)

An unknown God offers to the leader of a nomadic clan a new future, a future as wide as the world. This God promises him a blessing, in other words a gift of greater life. At the same time, God asks for Abraham's co-operation so that this new type of existence might become a reality: 'Go from your country ...'. And so it came about that, in the midst of human history, something began to change: 'So Abram went, as the Lord had told him ...' (Gen 12.4a).

The Jewish and Christian tradition has seen,

behind this act of Abraham, a basic attitude that represents the foundation of the relationship between human beings and their God. St Paul is the one who sets it out most clearly:

Just as Abraham 'had faith in God, and it was reckoned to him as righteousness' (Gen 15.6), know then that all who live lives of faith are children of Abraham. . . . all who live lives of faith are blessed with Abraham the man of faith.
(Gal 3.6–9; cf. Rom 4.1ff.; Heb 11.8ff.; 1 Macc 2.52)

More basic than any act human beings can perform is thus the attitude of trust by which they open the depths of their heart to God and welcome the new reality which they are offered. This inner movement of trust and welcome, which Paul calls faith, naturally takes concrete shape in particular acts, as was already the case for Abraham (cf. James 2.18–23), but it goes much further. It makes a human being a partner worthy of God, in biblical language, a righteous man or woman (cf. Wis 10.5).

It goes without saying that an attitude of this sort has nothing automatic about it. Human beings do not find it easy to live centred on a reality which is beyond their ken and their control. Being open to the unknown, with no securities near at hand, makes us vulnerable, an extremely uncomfortable position for beings who are ill-disposed to surrender the reins of their autonomy and always ready to settle down happily and live in a closed world, provided the necessary diversions are available.

As we follow the biblical account we discover that, more often than not, people are unable to enter into the unsettling adventure which God sets before them. In fact, it is quite possible to read Scripture as the story of the various ways in which human beings reject God's project, to see the Bible as an epic of lack of trust. Let us now look at some of the reasons for this refusal to trust, not in order to fall prey to discouragement, but so as better to discern the nature and the consequences of faith in God.

Just after the account of his calling, we read that Abraham goes down to Egypt. His vulnerable situation leads him to try and pass off his wife Sarah for his sister, in order to save his skin (Gen 12.10–20). It is Pharaoh himself (!) who has to show him the folly of trying to save himself by his own wiles rather than by trusting in God.

In fact Abraham, and his contemporaries who people the book of Genesis, have to undergo a whole process of learning what trust is all about. This culminates for Abraham in the dramatic story of the sacrifice of Isaac, recapitulated in those magnificent words 'the Lord will provide' (Gen 22). More classical examples of the difficulties of believing come from the Exodus story, however. When God sends Moses to the Israelites to announce their imminent liberation, we read that

Moses told this to the Israelites; but they would not listen to Moses, because of their broken spirit and their cruel slavery.

(Exod 6.9)

The people have suffered too much; they no longer dare to hope in a better future. Here despair, the attitude of someone who has been beaten down once too often, becomes the obstacle to trusting in God. And who can say they have not known such a day of darkness, when disappointment made it almost impossible to believe that one day the sun would shine again?

Nonetheless, in spite of the people's refusal to believe, God liberates them from their captors in Egypt. And now another difficulty faces them: between the land of oppression and their new life lies the arduous crossing of the desert. In this place of deprivation the Israelites, tormented by fear of the unknown and the perils of the journey, lose their confidence in God and want to turn back:

The whole congregation of the Israelites complained against Moses and Aaron in the wilderness. The Israelites said to them, 'If only we had died by the hand of the Lord in the land of Egypt ... ' (...) The people thirsted there for water; and the people complained against Moses and said, 'Why did you bring us out of Egypt, to kill us and our children and livestock with thirst?' (...) 'Why is the Lord bringing us into this land to fall by the sword? Our wives and our little ones will become booty; would it not be better for us to go back to Egypt?' So they said to one another, 'Let us choose a captain, and go back to Egypt.'

(Exod 16.2–3a; 17.3; Num 14.3–4)

These doubts about God, whose intentions are now distorted, are reinforced by a failure of memory, by a nostalgic vision of the land of slavery:

We remember the fish we used to eat in Egypt for nothing, the cucumbers, the melons, the leeks, the onions, and the garlic; but now our strength is dried up, and there is nothing at all but this manna to look at.

(Num 11.5–6)

Here too, who has not experienced in their moments of uncertainty and suffering nostalgia for 'the good old days', the temptation to find solace in an illusory past?

This lack of trust culminates in the story of the golden calf (Exod 32). Frightened by the disappearance of Moses, the people ask Aaron, 'Make gods for us, who shall go before us' (Exod 32.1), gods easy to see and to 'follow', because they are made in the people's own image. The roots of idolatry are thus clearly indicated: a flight from the discomforts of the new and the attempt to replace trust in God by security in things which can be controlled.

But fear and suffering are not the only things that can call into question an attitude of faith in God; paradoxically, the very same thing can occur when life is too easy. In the book of Deuteronomy, Moses explains this to the people on the eve of their entry into the promised land:

For the Lord your God is bringing you into a good land, a land with flowing streams, . . . a land of wheat and barley, of vines and fig trees, . . . where you will lack nothing . . .
Take care that you do not forget the Lord your God by failing to keep his commandments, his ordinances, and his statutes, which I am commanding you today. When you have eaten your fill and have built fine houses and live in them, and when your herds and flocks have multiplied, and your silver and gold is multiplied, and all that you have is multiplied, then do not exalt yourself . . . Do not say to yourself, 'My power and the might of my own hand have gotten me this wealth.' But remember the Lord your God . . .

(Deut 8.7–18)

At the time when the definitive version of this book was composed, the nation had undoubtedly been living for some time already in the land of Canaan.

Moses' words, therefore, are not a simple warning regarding the future but a reflection based on concrete experiences: as soon as the people settle in the promised land and their situation begins to improve, they begin to live a 'settled' life that makes trust in God more and more superfluous.

Fortunately, in this situation Israel is not left to its own devices. When the people God has formed, lulled to sleep in this way by a settled existence, begins to forget the source of its life, individuals arise to remind it of the need to trust in the Lord of the unexpected. These individuals are the beings of fire we know as the *prophets*. One of them, Isaiah of Jerusalem, reprimands the nation one day for its superficial piety (Isa 29.13). He tells his contemporaries that, because they are not rooted in trust in the God who comes to do something new, the ongoing activity of that God in history can only leave them perplexed:

> So I will again do amazing things with this people,
> shocking and amazing.
> The wisdom of their wise shall perish,
> and the discernment of the discerning shall be hidden.
> (Isa 29.14)

On another occasion, the prophet sharply criticizes Israel's search for security, in a time of political instability, through alliances with powerful neighbours, notably Egypt (Isa 31.1ff.). It is as if everyone had forgotten that, in days gone by, Pharaoh's entire army was unsuccessful in battle against God.

A century later, Jerusalem once again faces a threat of invasion. Another prophet, Jeremiah, when confronted with the people's facile confidence that all will be well because of the presence in their midst of the 'Lord's house', the Temple, does not hesitate even to attack this institution, one of the most sacred in Israel (Jer 7.1–15). Jeremiah has nothing against the Temple itself; what he combats is the folly of finding one's security there instead of in trying to act in a way pleasing to God. He realizes that God can never become a possession; the only way to maintain a relationship with God is by a trust that tears us away from our all-too-human certainties. And unfortunately for those who do put their trust in the building, soon afterwards the nation is invaded by the Babylonians, the city and its Temple destroyed and the nation's rulers taken into captivity. For those who mistook these expressions for the source of their faith, nothing was left standing.

Questions for Reflection

1. What realities in my life are in danger of becoming an obstacle to trust in God? Where am I threatened by the temptation of a 'settled' life? How can I discover again and again what is truly essential?

2. What form can the temptation to nostalgia take for us? How can we see the past instead as a wellspring that gives courage and vitality in the present?

3. Read Psalm 106. According to its author, what is the basic attitude of the people throughout their history? Why does the psalm say that Moses 'stood in the breach before them' (v. 23)? Why, in spite of everything, does it invite the nation to 'give thanks to the Lord' (v. 1)?

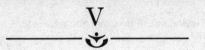

V

AN ONGOING CREATION

A T A time when the fortunes of the nation were at their lowest ebb, in the land of captivity a prophet arose who understood God's identity and activity more clearly than anyone else up to that time. That anonymous prophet, usually referred to as Second Isaiah because his words are found in the second part of the book of Isaiah (chapters 40–55), speaks to a defeated people who are tempted to cling nostalgically to a bygone era. In order to enter into the outlook of his contemporaries, this prophet speaks in his turn of the marvels accomplished by the Lord centuries ago during the Exodus from Egypt:

> Thus says the Lord, who makes a way in the sea,
> a path in the mighty waters,
> who brings out chariot and horse, army and warrior;
> they lie down, they cannot rise,
> they are extinguished, quenched like a wick ...
>
> (Isa 43.16–17)

But then the prophet goes on to pronounce in God's name these words, as unexpected as they are disconcerting:

> Do not remember the former things,
> or consider the things of old.

> I am about to do a new thing;
> now it springs forth, do you not perceive it?
> I will make a way in the wilderness ...
>
> (Isa 43.18–19a)

Second Isaiah calls his contemporaries to a change of outlook: stop clinging to the past, look at what God is doing *now*! The prophet has realized that the very same God who freed the people long ago is the one who is still present in order to perform a miracle of the same order here and now, in the present moment.

For all that, this prophet is far from being a revolutionary who wishes to wipe out the past and rebuild the nation upon entirely new foundations. He does not mean to discourage his contemporaries from reflecting upon what the Lord has done in the course of their history. We have just seen that he himself does not hesitate to speak of the Exodus, and he consciously walks in the footsteps of the prophets who went before him. But for Second Isaiah, all that went before is in the service of the living God who is coming *now* to do a new thing. While taking a firm stand against the flight to nostalgia, the prophet encourages his compatriots to 'remember' (Isa 44.21) what the Lord did in the past, in order to discern more clearly God's presence in the present day.

Better than any other part of the Hebrew Scriptures, Isaiah 40 – 55 helps us understand how the two themes of newness and continuity come together in God. What often strikes us as polar opposites are found to be, in God, two sides of one and the same coin. God is by definition the One who is always present for believers, and always the same. But God is present precisely as the One who offers a new life, a life beyond all imagining: God is the One who comes to do something new. If we look at history in order to discover the 'marvels' God accomplished in the past, to discern a continuity in God's acts, this makes us more able to understand how God is at work in our lives here and now. Similarly, the Lord's past interventions are never over and done with: they participate in his everlasting newness. They are inexhaustible 'wellsprings' we can return to over and over again, sources of trust that inspire and nourish us today, tomorrow and always.

What, in Second Isaiah's eyes, is the 'new thing' that God is about to do for the Israelites far from home? First of all, the prophet describes it using the image of a highway in the wilderness (Isa 43.19; cf. 40.3; 42.16; 49.11). In other words, a road is going to open up for the exiles' return home: it will be a kind of 'new Exodus', more impressive than the first one (Isa 40.10–11; 49.9–13; 51.11; 52.7–12; 55.12). But in speaking of the marvellous and unexpected deed which God is about to accomplish, Second Isaiah employs an even more significant cluster of images:

> I will make a way in the wilderness
> and rivers in the desert.
> The wild animals will honour me,
> the jackals and the ostriches;
> for I give water in the wilderness,
> rivers in the desert,
> to give drink to my chosen people.
>
> (Isa 43.19b–20)

Springs of water will gush forth and the desert will become a garden:

> I will put in the wilderness the cedar,
> the acacia, the myrtle, and the olive;
> I will set in the desert the cypress,
> the plane and the pine together ...
>
> (Isa 41.19)

And the following verse explains the meaning of these images:

> ... so that all may see and know,
> all may consider and understand,
> that the hand of the Lord has done this,
> the Holy One of Israel has *created* it.
>
> (Isa 41.20)

'The Holy One of Israel has created it.' For anyone at all familiar with the world of the Bible, these images evoke the accounts of the creation of the world 'in the beginning' (cf. Gen 2.4b–10). As a matter of fact, this prophet refers several times to God as Creator of the universe (Isa 40.26, 28; 42.5; 45.7, 18), of human beings (Isa 45.12), and of Israel (Isa 43.1, 7, 15). The Hebrew verb 'to create' has a very strong meaning: always used with God alone as subject, it describes an act of divine omnipotence by which something brand-new arises out of nothing. The surprising thing, then, is that Second Isaiah uses this notion to speak not of what went on in some distant past but of what God is accomplishing here and now:

> From this time forward I make you hear new things,
> hidden things that you have not known.
> They are created now, not long ago ...
>
> (Isa 48.6b–7a)

Here we glimpse, in its full scope, the biblical doctrine of creation. God is not the Creator simply because of something done long ago, at the beginning of time. No, God is always the Creator; it is part of the divine nature to bring something new into being. Second Isaiah clearly understood that God's creative activity is at work throughout the course of history. This is shown in the following oracle, which speaks in the same breath of the creation of the universe (described here in mythical terms as a struggle with the personified forces of chaos), the crossing of the sea during the Exodus from Egypt, and the 'new Exodus', the return from Babylon:

> Awake, awake, put on strength,
> O arm of the Lord!
> Awake, as in days of old,
> the generations of long ago!
> Was it not you who cut Rahab in pieces,
> who pierced the dragon?
> Was it not you who dried up the sea,
> the waters of the great deep;
> who made the depths of the sea a way
> for the redeemed to cross over?
> So the ransomed of the Lord shall return,
> and come to Zion with singing;
> everlasting joy shall be upon their heads;
> they shall obtain joy and gladness,
> and sorrow and sighing shall flee away.
>
> (Isa 51.9–11)

The 'arm of the Lord' that does these wonders is at the origin both of the creation of the world and of all God's creative interventions throughout history. It is not surprising, then, that when a disciple of Second Isaiah wants to express a hope for the future, he explains that God is going to 'create new heavens and a new earth' (Isa 65.17).

And now, how does Second Isaiah view the human *response* to the God who comes to continue the work of creation by saving his people from captivity? First of all, the prophet encourages his compatriots to be open to what the Lord is doing in the present moment. That means turning away from the flight to a nostalgic past (Isa 43.18) and not being impressed by the so-called gods of Babylon (Isa 44.9ff.), in order to return to God (Isa 44.22) by listening confidently (Isa 42.18, 23 etc.) to the 'good news' (cf. Isa 52.7) of what the Lord is about to accomplish. In other words, the prophet preaches a *conversion* of the entire being, a step that is essential in order to enter into the project of the One who comes to do something new.

Once human beings have entered into this process of conversion, a second and more important stage can begin:

> See, the former things have come to pass,
> and new things I now declare;
> before they spring forth,
> I tell you of them.
> Sing to the Lord a new song,
> his praise from the end of the earth!
> Let the sea roar and all that fills it,
> the coastlands and their inhabitants ...
> (Isa 42.9–10)

In the eyes of the prophet, the only response worthy of God and his marvellous deeds is, in the final analysis, the bringing to birth of a 'new song' (cf. Ps 98.1; Rev 5.9; 14.3). The expression does not refer to some melody previously unknown: the song is new because it arises from hearts and lips penetrated and transformed by the 'new thing' God is doing. And it is not even limited to human voices but has a cosmic dimension, or as many would say today an ecological one: the entire universe is invited to take part in an explosion of joy and praise that marks the coming of the God who makes all things new (Isa 44.23; 49.13; 55.12).

Questions for Reflection

In Isaiah 44.21–23, the prophet enumerates three responses to the activity of God: remember, return, sing and shout.

1. Have I ever experienced moments of intensity when, for an instant, the clouds dispersed and I was able to grasp something about God? How can I keep such experiences alive to help me in the present moment?

2. What is the reason for the prophet's conviction that it is always possible to return to God? What makes us able to believe in God's forgiveness?

3. Concretely, how can we sing a new song in our lives?

VI

THE WAYS OF THE SPIRIT

IN ONE of the oracles in which Second Isaiah speaks of the 'new thing' brought about by the Lord, we find these words:

> ... I will pour water on the thirsty land,
> and streams on the dry ground;
> I will pour my spirit upon your descendants,
> and my blessing on your offspring.
>
> (Isa 44.3)

Here the new act of creation, described as a gift of water in the desert (cf. Gen 2.6), is explained as a blessing from God and an outpouring of the divine *ruah*, the breath or spirit of God. The biblical notion of the Spirit shows itself to be an important language to express God's newness. It is worthwhile, therefore, to try and understand better the evolution of this idea in the Hebrew Scriptures.

In many of the world's religious traditions, we encounter the notion of *possession*: the behaviour of a human being is transformed as a result of a supernatural presence — benevolent or malevolent — that takes control of him or her. In ancient Israel, it seems that the origins of the prophetic movement were associated with this phenomenon. The first 'prophets' we encounter in the Bible are itinerant bands of seers, poor (2 Kings 4.1, 38) and despised (1 Sam 10.11–12; 2 Kings 9.11), who fall into a trance to the accompaniment of sacred music. When Samuel, for example, responds to the Israelites' request by choosing Saul to be their leader and anointing him as king (1 Sam 10), he explains to the new king that, among the signs that will show that God is with him, the following event will occur:

... as you come to the town, you will meet a band of prophets coming down from the shrine with harp, tambourine, flute, and lyre playing in front of them; they will be in a prophetic frenzy. Then the spirit of the Lord will possess you, and you will be in a prophetic frenzy along with them and be turned into a different person.

(1 Sam 10.5–6)

In this age-old text, the Spirit of God manifests itself by suddenly taking possession of a human being in a rather violent fashion; it is understood as a divine reality that endows a person — provisionally — with a new form of behaviour. Saul is 'turned into a different person'. It is worth noting that here the Spirit's presence is disclosed by obvious external signs, sometimes rather bizarre ones (cf. 1 Sam 19.24).

In the final version of this story, however, what interests the author is not so much the 'ecstatic' or abnormal aspect of things as the fact that the presence of the Spirit, linked to the anointing, is a confirmation that God is the one who has chosen Saul to lead the people (1 Sam 10.1). This is, in fact, the main function attributed to the Spirit of God by the Hebrew Scriptures: by means of the Spirit, the Lord personally sets apart human beings to do his work, in this way giving them a new mission, and even a new identity.

This is shown even more clearly when Saul's successor, the great king David, is chosen: 'Then Samuel took the horn of oil, and anointed him in the presence of his brothers; and the spirit of the Lord came mightily upon David from that day forward' (1 Sam 16.13). The Hebrew Scriptures contain many other examples where the Spirit is found at the origin of a vocation. The Spirit's presence is mentioned, for instance, in the book of Judges to explain the activity of the *shofetim* ('judges'), those provisional leaders who, in the early days after the settlement in Canaan, took charge of the people in times of crisis (e.g. Judg 3.10; 6.34). Similarly, in the final version of the books of Moses, we are told that the seventy elders can share Moses' authority only because they have received 'the spirit that was on him' (Num 11.16–30). And later on, when the kings are unfaithful to God and the great prophets arise to point out the way of the Lord to their contemporaries, they likewise claim the assistance of God's Spirit (Micah 3.8; Ezek 2.2; 11.5; cf. 2 Chron 15.1; Zech 7.12; 2 Pet 1.21).

When we come to the prophets, however, we encounter a problem that will always haunt those who claim to possess the Spirit of God. This problem is clearly illustrated in chapter 22 of the first book of Kings. The king of Israel wants to wage war. All but one of the prophets he consults tell him to go ahead; that one, however, warns him that it is not God's will. What is to be done when the prophets do not agree among themselves? How can we know who is truly inspired by God? Here, the theme of the *discernment of spirits* makes its appearance; gradually, it will be understood that all inspiration does not necessarily come from the Spirit of God. Other 'spirits' may be at work, and thus a process of discernment is called for.

As a matter of fact, perhaps in part because of this difficulty, some of the great prophets hardly refer to the Spirit at all. A man like Jeremiah speaks more about the *Word* of God: 'The Word of the Lord came to me saying ... '. Word implies message, content; words can be verified by comparing them to other words spoken by other prophets in the past and thus, little by little, a tradition takes shape. This points the way to one solution to the problem of discernment. It is therefore of the utmost importance that the Spirit should not be separated from the Word, and the Bible in fact often keeps the two in close contact.

In addition to referring to God's Spirit to explain the transformation or calling of a human being, the Hebrew Scriptures also speak of the Spirit as the Creator's life-breath that is the source of being and life. In chapter 2 of the book of Genesis (Gen 2.4ff.) we find a second account of the creation of the world, apparently more ancient than the first one (Gen 1). The author employs the image of a desert to which God brings water, turning it into a garden (Gen 2.4b–6, 8–10). Then he describes the Lord as a potter who fashions the human being (*adam*) from the earth (*adamah*) (Gen 2.7a). But with this the act of creation is not yet completed: '[God] breathed into his nostrils the breath of life; and the man became a living being' (Gen 2.7b). Even if human beings share a kinship with the earth, to be truly themselves they must receive directly from the Creator this gift of a breath of life.

To grasp the significance of this age-old story, we must avoid seeing it in terms of our own modern categories and concerns. The author is unfamiliar with our distinctions between the Holy Spirit, the human spirit and even the act of breathing. What he affirms with force and art is that the human being is unique, a creature unlike all others, created by the encounter between two realities: the dust of the earth and the breath or spirit that comes from God.* Similarly, in Psalm 104.29–30, the author sees creation as a continuous process by which life and death follow one another rhythmically as God gives and then takes back his breath.

Finding the Spirit in the first account of the creation (Gen 1) is not as easy as it might at first seem. The passage begins with these words: ' . . . a divine *ruah* swept over the face of the waters' (Gen 1.2). The word *ruah* can also mean 'wind', and so some translators see here only a mighty wind, one of the aspects of the primeval chaos. But the verb 'to sweep, hover' is found elsewhere in the Bible only in Deuteronomy 32.11, a text in which God is compared to an eagle watching over its young. And both the Jewish and Christian tradition has most often seen in this verse an allusion to God's Spirit preparing the *tohu-bohu*, the primeval chaos, to welcome God's Word. Creation would thus be the work of 'the two hands of God', as St Irenaeus puts it, the Spirit and the Word. This same collaboration, incidentally, is indicated in Psalm 33.6: 'By the word of the Lord the heavens

---

*It should be pointed out that the Hebrew word translated by 'breath of life' in Gen 2.7b is not *ruah* but *nishmah*, a synonym.

were made, and all their host by the breath of his mouth.'

Finally, the Spirit is presented, less frequently, as the divine presence that guides or leads human beings. In Isaiah 63.7ff., the prophet affirms that the Lord's Spirit led the people during the Exodus from Egypt. And to characterize the refusal to follow God's ways, he uses the expression: 'they grieved his Holy Spirit' (Isa 63.10; cf. Eph 4.30). The Wisdom literature, in turn, sometimes speaks of an inner 'inspiration' that sets people on the right road (Job 32.8; cf. Prov 20.27); the ability to distinguish good from evil is thus seen as coming from the Spirit of God. The Lord's Spirit: wellspring of life, means of transformation, guiding presence ... Far from offering us a systematic doctrine regarding this manifestation of God, the Scriptures of the people of Israel present instead fragments of revelation glimpsed in this or that particular situation. The Spirit is virtually never considered in and for itself, to such an extent that it would not be wrong to see this discretion as a positive characteristic of the Spirit's identity.

But one thing already stands out clearly, and it is the exact opposite of the way modern people view the world. For us, so-called 'spiritual' realities — and by extension the Spirit — are less real than material things, less solid, more fleeting. For the Bible the reverse is true: while 'the flesh' is weak (Matt 26.41) like the grass that quickly withers and dies (Isa 40.6–8), the Spirit is force, vitality, energy; it shares in the eternal and inexhaustible dynamism of the Creator God (cf. Isa 31.3; 40.26–31).

Questions for Reflection

1. Faith is not merely obedience to an external reality but openness to an inner Presence. How do the texts of the Bible that speak of the Holy Spirit help us to understand this truth?

2. How can we learn to distinguish inspirations that come to us from God from those that come from somewhere else? What can we learn about this from the following texts: 1 John 4.1–6; 1 Thessalonians 5.19–21; Galatians 5.22–23; Romans 14.17–19; Ephesians 4.30–32?

VII

TOWARDS A NEW WORLD

A T A critical moment in the existence of his people, the anonymous prophet of the Exile went back to the sources of Israel's religious heritage to restore confidence to his demoralized contemporaries. His meditation on the past provided courage for the present and hope for the future, because it was rooted in a God who is an eternal source of newness, a Creator God.

It is significant that the difficulties of the present brought out more clearly the dimension of biblical faith open to the future, a dimension somewhat underplayed during the centuries of settled life in Palestine. In those times of relative tranquillity, the aspect of *promise* so characteristic of the faith of Abraham receded into the background; the prophets' field of vision was occupied primarily by the dangers of forgetting the Lord and replacing God, for all practical purposes, by human forms of security.

With the Exile, however, the promise once again became a focus of attention. The centuries just before the Christian era saw the awakening of an intense longing for a new, definitive intervention of God. Believers were ardently awaiting a manifestation of God's presence that would heal the wounds of human history and bring the fullness of life to the faithful who were being cruelly tried.

At the same time, it is important to realize that no consensus existed regarding when and how this new divine intervention would take place. The biblical and prophetic texts generally express the longing for God's coming in an allusive manner, by means of images. How can 'what no eye has seen, nor ear has heard' (1 Cor 2.9; cf. Isa 64.3) be adequately expressed in words? We are thus confronted by a multiplicity of languages, not explicitly harmonized among themselves.

In the last chapter we saw that, for Second Isaiah, the 'new creation' which God accomplished by liberating the people from captivity and leading them home involved a descent of the Holy Spirit: 'I will pour my spirit upon your descendants' (Isa 44.3). If God is the Creator — the Being whose nature it is to bring about something new — and if God creates by means of his Spirit, then it is not surprising that the hope proclaimed by the prophets is often linked to a new coming of the Creator Spirit into the world. So, for example, this other text from the book of Isaiah:

> ... until a spirit from on high is poured out for us,
> and the wilderness becomes a fruitful field,
> and the fruitful field is deemed a forest.
> Then justice will dwell in the wilderness,
> and righteousness abide in the fruitful field.
> The effect of righteousness will be peace,
> and the result of righteousness,
> quietness and trust forever.
> My people will abide in a peaceful habitation,
> in secure dwellings, and in quiet resting places.
>
> (Isa 32.15–18)

The text begins with the image, already by now a traditional one, of a desert that is changed into fertile land. By means of the Spirit, God takes up the work of creation again. But it quickly becomes evident that this image has above all a symbolic value. The 'new creation' goes further than the previous one, and takes place on a different level. Here it is a question of the establishment of a world of justice and peace.

At another time, during the first deportations of the conquered Jews to Babylon, the prophet Ezekiel likewise saw the link between the Spirit of God and the fulfilment of the promise. In a vision, God shows him a valley filled with dry bones (Ezek 37.1–14). When the prophet proclaims the Word of God to these bones, they join together to form human bodies. Then he receives the command to call upon the Spirit, and suddenly the bodies come to life. The message is clear: the same God who created the world from the dust of the earth (cf. Gen 2.4b–7) can repeat the miracle of creation for his exhausted and demoralized people, by means of the Word and the Spirit.

Elsewhere, Ezekiel shows more clearly how this re-creation will come about. He has understood the necessity for the nation, if it is to correspond to what God expects of it, to be transformed inwardly. And this transformation will be the work of the Spirit, who will give the people a new heart, docile to impulses coming from God (Ezek 36.26–27). Ezekiel thus takes up and develops the prophecy of his predecessor Jeremiah concerning the new covenant (Jer 31.31–34), a time when the Torah will be written on people's hearts, in other words internalized as a motivating force for life. The prophet Joel, in turn, says the same thing in another way: he looks forward to a time when the Spirit will be poured out upon 'all flesh', so that everyone will become in essence a prophet, capable of discerning God's will (Joel 2.28–29).

According to other prophetic oracles, the world to come will be inaugurated by someone sent from God for this purpose — a king like David, a prophet like Elijah, or perhaps a new Moses. This figure is sometimes given the title of 'Messiah', the Anointed One: to accomplish his mission, it goes without saying that he must benefit from the aid of the Spirit of God (Isa 11.1–9; 42.1–4; 61.1–4).

This survey of texts in which Israel looks towards the future is far from being exhaustive. It attempts simply to show that, when the Bible attempts to put into words a hope, the Spirit plays an important role. The presence of the Spirit is a kind of guarantee that we are dealing with a new creative intervention of God. The return of the Spirit, present 'in the beginning', is the sign that we have come full circle, that the time of fulfilment has arrived. In fact, eventually the Spirit will become the basic content of the Bible's hope: St Luke refers to the Spirit simply as 'what the Father has promised' (Luke 24.49; Acts 1.4; cf. Acts 2.33; Eph 1.13).

Questions for Reflection

1. What can we do to keep alive in us the dimension of longing, of expectation, so characteristic of biblical faith? How can we allow hope in God to transform and deepen our human hopes?
2. In times of discouragement, which men and

women have been for me living signs that a different future is possible?

3. Read Isaiah 11.1–9; 42.1–4; 61.1–4. These texts draw a kind of preliminary sketch of the one who is to come to inaugurate a new world. What do they tell us about the activity of this figure? What role does the Holy Spirit play in his life? In what way does the life of Jesus correspond to these portraits?

PART TWO

IN THE DYNAMISM OF THE SPIRIT
Luke 4.14

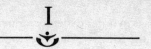
WELCOMING THE GOOD NEWS

TO GRASP the full relevance of 'the Good News of Jesus, the Messiah, the Son of God' (Mark 1.1), it must be read in the light of this centuries-long and many-sided longing of Israel, which had become particularly acute in the period following the Exile. For, from the very beginning, the disciples of Jesus were convinced of one thing:

In the old days God spoke in many different ways to our ancestors through the prophets; now, in the final days, he has spoken to us through his Son.

(Heb 1.1–2a)

Jesus inaugurates the 'final days', in other words, with him human history reaches its great turning-point, characterized by the fullness of revelation. The New Testament does not call into question the fact that the mystery of God has been revealed in many different shapes and forms throughout the ages. But it insists that Christ recapitulates what was incomplete or fragmentary in the other revelations and responds to the longings that were implicit in them. To put it in the language of this book, the newness of Christ is that of restoring, unifying, completing and fulfilling beyond all expectations what has already been given. If it leads to a break with the past, this is in order to demonstrate, from the vantage point of the future, a more profound continuity.

If this is the case, then it follows that what we have already discovered concerning the identity of God and the Spirit will find in the life of Christ a surprising confirmation and deepening. Let us begin by following the thread of the gospel which many consider to be the oldest and which is in any case the least cluttered, the gospel according to St Mark.

At the beginning of Mark's gospel, we encounter the figure of John the Baptist. By his words and his actions, and even by the clothes he wears, John resembles a prophet of a bygone era (Mark 1.4–6). In fact, we can see in him the best, the quintessence, of the faith of ancient Israel. His appearance generates much enthusiasm (Mark 1.5) and gives rise to the question 'Are you the one we are waiting for?' (cf. John 1.19–22). He replies by speaking of someone else, greater than him: 'I have baptized you with water, but he will baptize you with the Holy Spirit' (Mark 1.8). In other words, by means of this 'other one', the longing for a new outpouring of the creative and prophetic Spirit of God to transform the world will finally be fulfilled.

What a surprise, then, to see Jesus come as a penitent and ask John to baptize *him* (Mark 1.9)! Here we already encounter a basic theme of the Gospel: the One sent by God comes to inaugurate the new age, but not, as is expected, through a kind of spectacular overthrow of the present order (cf. Luke 3.16–17). On the contrary, he comes simply and discreetly, in an act of solidarity with humanity that has turned away from God. And immediately we are given a confirmation that we are in fact witnessing a new creation: the heavens open, God acclaims Jesus as his beloved Son and the Spirit descends upon him to 'remain' (Mark 1.10–11; John 1.32). The mention of the 'dove' to characterize this presence of the Spirit emphasizes the theme of a new beginning; we find it in the story of Noah, to mark the end of the old order washed away in the great flood (Gen 8.8–12), and in the Song of Solomon, to symbolize the end of winter and the blossoming of springtime (Song 2.12).

But then there come these surprising words: 'At once the Spirit drives Jesus into the wilderness [where he was] put to the test by Satan' (Mark 1.12–13). The Spirit leads Jesus into those regions where God seems absent, to places of death and of trials. Once again, it becomes clear that the coming of a renewed world can only occur through an act of solidarity with the human condition in all its dimensions, down to and including its lowest depths, so that nothing at all will be excluded from the transforming presence of God.

After this preparation, we witness the beginnings of Jesus' mission (Mark 1.14). John disappears abruptly from the scene as if to mark the end of one historical period, and Jesus *comes*. Already in itself the mere use of this simple verb of movement by the evangelist is eloquent: the God of the Bible is the God who comes to human beings to do something new, and Jesus thus, from the outset, takes his place in this same great movement. Jesus comes not to communicate a philosophy of life or ideas about God, but to 'announce some good news'. The Greek word *euangelion* ('good news, gospel') always refers to an event that changes the course of history. Second

Isaiah used it to speak of the new thing God was about to do in liberating the people from captivity:

> How beautiful upon the mountains
> are the feet of the messenger who announces peace,
> who brings good news,
> who announces salvation,
> who says to Zion, 'Your God reigns'.

(Isa 52.7)

And Jesus takes up the same language to express the core of his own good news:

The time has come and the Reign of God is at hand: change your hearts and believe in the good news!

(Mark 1.15)

In both cases we have the announcement of a unique event ('good news') which will show that God is in charge of history and the universe (God 'reigns'). The relationship between these two texts emphasizes the fact that Jesus, far from transmitting a theoretical doctrine about God, comes in order to bear witness to a new presence of the Creator, now active at the heart of creation to bring his work to completion. St Luke, always attentive to the presence of the Holy Spirit in Jesus, explains here that Jesus comes 'in the power (*dynamis*) of the Spirit' (Luke 4.14; cf. 4.1). And in Luke's gospel, Jesus begins his ministry by reading aloud in the synagogue of Nazareth the text of Isaiah 61 ('The Spirit of the Lord is upon me ...') and applying it to himself.

Even before telling us any more about this new presence of God that he communicates in the dynamism of the Spirit, Jesus explains that it requires a radical response from those who encounter it:

'change your hearts and believe'. In other words, the hearers are invited to place their trust in the messenger, to take his message seriously and let it transform their lives from beginning to end. It is less a question of outward steps to take than of an inner movement of welcome, of openness, repeated again and again, in order to allow the newness of God to enter the world by means of consenting hearts.

Nevertheless, as if to warn us that the emphasis on inner openness does not at all imply passivity, the following verses show how the proclamation and the response take concrete shape in the lives of a few ordinary people. Like their ancestor Abraham before them, four simple fishermen undertake a radical new beginning in the company of Christ. They leave family, home and work to set out on an adventure with him (Mark 1.16–20).

Questions for Reflection

1. Why does John the Baptist hesitate to baptize Jesus (Matt 3.14)? What is the meaning of Jesus' reply (Matt 3.15)?

2. What does John want to express by applying the text of Isaiah 40.3 to himself (John 1.23)? How does his example help us to understand the calling of a believer and the secret of perfect joy (John 3.27–30)? How can we let Christ grow in us?

3. In Matthew 4.1–11 and Luke 4.1–13, Jesus' trials in the wilderness are shown in detail. The Tempter tries to shake his faith, to weaken his trust in his Father. What do we learn by comparing these stories with the journey of the Israelites in the desert after the Exodus (see e.g. Exod 15.22 – 16.3; Num

20.1–11)? How can we in our turn cope with the trials that threaten the faith of every believer?

4. The baptism of Jesus is an example of the fact that what was promised as a result of the definitive intervention of God does not come about in the way human beings expect it. What other examples of this fundamental truth of faith do we find in the gospels?

II

WORDS OF POWER, ACTS OF HEALING

IN WHAT exactly does the new presence of God announced by Jesus consist? How does the fullness of the Spirit manifest itself in him? If Jesus never gives us any explicit definition of these realities, the reason is quite simple: the answer to these questions is the whole of his existence. Each of his words and each of his acts, and above all the end of his life, allow us to penetrate more deeply into the mystery of the Reign of God. There is no other road than this — to trust in him and to follow him step by step on his journey.

In the text from the book of Isaiah which Jesus reads at the beginning of his ministry (Luke 4.18ff.), the presence of the Spirit is shown first of all in an act of speaking: 'to *announce* good news to the poor . . . to *proclaim* liberation to captives'. We have already noted the close link in the Bible between the Spirit-Breath and the (spoken) Word. Now we are in a better position to understand why the first thing that strikes people is 'that [Jesus] was teaching them like someone possessing authority, and not like the scribes' (Mark 1.22). Jesus possesses an inner authority which comes from God's Spirit. His words, like those spoken by God at the creation of the universe (cf. Gen 1), bring about what they announce; they even have the power to overcome the forces of evil

(Mark 1.23–26). That is why Mark presents Jesus' teaching and his exorcisms as a single reality (Mark 1.27).

Jesus spends much time teaching the crowds in general and his disciples in particular. He does not wish to treat human beings as passive robots: they are called to enter consciously and voluntarily into the new life he comes to offer. This feature distinguishes the 'new creation' from the creation of the universe 'in the beginning': the former cannot take place without the collaboration of human beings, without a personal commitment.

No teacher can escape the pedagogical dilemma of having to lead her pupils, beginning from what they already know, to a place they have not yet been. In order to do this, the teacher must find a language that points beyond itself. This dilemma is particularly acute for Jesus. How can our old worn-out words express the astounding newness of God, a reality utterly beyond any concepts or expressions native to the world here below? Jesus, deeply rooted in the Source of all meaning, finds solutions as if by instinct: he borrows images from daily life, he tells stories to make people think, he forges paradoxical expressions that are a kind of invitation to search further. In short, he does all he can so that the means of expression are not confused with the reality they are pointing to. Who could mistake a farmer sowing his field, or a woman who has lost some money, for the Ruler of the universe?

Some images used by Jesus, incidentally, deal with the problem we have just mentioned:

No one sews a piece of new cloth on an old garment, otherwise the new patch rips away from the old fabric, and the tear is even worse. And no one pours new wine into old wineskins, otherwise the wine causes the skins to burst, and both wine and wineskins are lost. No, new wine goes into new wineskins!

(Mark 2.21–22)

God's newness cannot simply take its place in the customary routine of a human life, like a trophy set on the mantelpiece. By its nature it tends rather to upset a settled existence, acting like a pinch of yeast that slowly but surely raises the entire loaf.

The acts by which Jesus heals the sick ('sight to the blind', Luke 4.18) and chases away the spirit of evil are likewise signs of the Spirit's presence at work in him to bring about the Reign of God (cf. Matt 12.28). They help us understand that he came to bring to human beings the fullness of life (cf. John 10.10). In Jesus, God's creative power shows itself to be victorious over the destructive forces of evil (cf. Mark 3.27).

Far from being feats of magic, the healings of Jesus invite the sick person's collaboration through a response of faith (Mark 5.34; Matt 13.58 etc.). In this way they reveal the unity of the human condition: the Bible is ill at ease with our hard-and-fast separations between the material, the moral and the spiritual. Signs of a universe restored and brought to perfection, these acts are at the same time only signs; in other words they point in a certain direction, but they are not themselves the means by which Jesus will bring about God's Reign. It could almost be said that for him they have above all a pedagogical value, in that they want to help people to go further along the road and deepen their understanding (cf. John 6.26–27).

In his encounter with a paralysed man in Capernaum, Jesus openly reveals the deeper significance of his cures (Mark 2.1–12). Confronted with the afflicted man, Jesus does not respond at first by healing him as expected; instead, he speaks these surprising words, 'My child, your sins are forgiven'. The physical healing only comes later, as if to tell us that, in the final analysis, a body restored to full health is the sign of an inner and deeper healing, known as the forgiveness of sins.

In fact, forgiveness, a healing of the roots of evil, is for Jesus one of the cornerstones of his message.* In a great programmatic discourse situated at the beginning of his ministry, Jesus speaks of two ways of living (Matt 5.38–48). One, the old one, characterizes human beings left to themselves: they love those who love them. They divide humanity into two categories, those who are with them and the others, and act in consequence. Jesus calls the other way of living, the new one, 'being perfect' (Matt 5.48): it is God's own way of being. And it is the road of forgiveness, on which one responds to hatred by love, to evil by doing good. Jesus takes up the biblical vision of a merciful God (cf. Exod 34.6; Ps 86.5, 15; 103.8) and shows just how far this goes. And he adds this astonishing corollary: from now on human beings can and

---

*It is significant that, in the speeches of Peter and Paul presented in the Acts of the Apostles as models of the apostolic preaching, forgiveness always occupies a prominent place. Cf. Acts 2.38; 5.31; 10.43; 13.38; 26.18.

must be truly in the image of God: 'Be merciful, as your Father is merciful' (Luke 6.36).

Do we understand why forgiveness is such an important aspect of the identity of the God of the Bible and, still more, of the Gospel? In these pages we are trying to show that the hallmark of God is that he is the Creator, the One who comes to do something new. But what is forgiveness if not a love that makes a new beginning possible, a love that recreates? For this reason true forgiveness — whether between God and human beings or between individuals or groups — is always a miracle. When it comes to liberate individuals or groups that were sinking into the quicksands of endless recriminations and mutual suspicion, forgiveness unmistakably brings a breath of fresh air that comes from somewhere else, from the One whose ways are not our ways (cf. Isa 55.6–9). Continuing to love those who are hostile or indifferent to us is not possible unless we are rooted in a source of energy, an inexhaustible wellspring that is not of this world.

Questions for Reflection

1. In the images and stories he takes from everyday life, Jesus often introduces an unexpected aspect that makes us stop and think. In the following texts, what image does Jesus use? Does it have an unexpected, or even shocking, aspect? How does it help us to grasp Jesus' message? Where do we see its relevance in our own life? Matthew 13.31–33; 18.1–4; Luke 14.7–14; 14.15–24; 15.1–7; John 3.1–8.
2. Jesus comes 'in the power of the Spirit'; in him God is fully at work. How do the following texts help

us to understand the consequences of this? Matthew 4.23–25; Luke 7.11–17; 9.10–17; John 8.1–11.

3. How does the call of Matthew and the meal at his home (Matt 9.9–13) enable us to understand the characteristics and the results of God's forgiveness?

III

RESISTANCE TO THE MESSAGE

AS LONG as life follows its pre-ordained course, we
can live with our eyes half-closed, or even as sleep-
walkers. But when something new occurs, we are
obliged to react, and sometimes to choose sides. It is
not surprising, then, that no one remains indifferent
to the coming of Jesus. The gospels show us a wide
range of possible responses: some leave everything
and follow him; others hesitate, or come to him in the
hope of benefiting themselves. And finally, astonishing as it may seem, there are those who reject his
message.

The gospel-writers show the beginnings of this
movement of refusal fairly early in the ministry of
Jesus. And the resistance seems to crystallize around
the question of forgiveness, around the revelation of a
God who loves everyone without exception.

In Mark's gospel, the first difficulty comes during
the healing of the paralysed man. Some of those
responsible for teaching the Torah do not want to
admit that Jesus has the authority to tell that unfortunate man that his sins are forgiven (Mark 2.6–7). And
afterwards, when Jesus makes this forgiveness tangible in the act of sharing a meal, a sign of fellowship,
with 'sinners', this scandalizes still further those who
identify themselves with the cause of God (Mark

2.15–17). In Jesus' activity on the sabbath day, these people do not see a life restored and renewed by God, and thus a revelation of the true significance of that Day, but a simple violation of the law (Mark 2.23 – 3.6). Blinded and burdened by what they have already attained, they are unable to see the new day that is beginning to dawn all around them (Mark 2.18–22; cf. John 9.39–41).

Seen in this setting, one of the most difficult texts in the entire gospel, the notorious 'blasphemy against the Holy Spirit' (Mark 3.22–30; Matt 12.22–32; Luke 11.14–23; 12.10), can receive clarification. Jesus' words do not in the least refer to some mysterious and specific act to be avoided at all costs, a 'sin' that, once committed, would place us definitively outside the realm of God's forgiveness. By its very nature, God's forgiveness has no such limits. But it is precisely this that Jesus' opponents refuse to recognize. Motivated by a jealousy that keeps them from seeing, in the words and acts of Jesus, the presence of God's Spirit creating a new world where all have their place, they attribute his work of healing and forgiveness to the spirit of evil. In Jesus' eyes, such a misunderstanding of God's identity by those who are supposed to know the Scriptures, God's revealed Word, is even more serious than their failure to recognize his own identity (Matt 12.32a). The obstinate refusal to open oneself to life and forgiveness in a certain sense ties God's hands, since love cannot impose itself by violating another's physical or spiritual integrity.[*]

*See explanatory note, p. 64.

When we read the gospels in their final version, there is a great temptation to judge Jesus' opponents harshly. Viewed with the benefit of hindsight they are easy targets, and by looking down on them we reinforce our own self-esteem. We enter more deeply into Jesus' outlook, however, when we realize that none of us are immune to the attitudes he criticizes. Some of the gospel stories are quite revealing in this regard. Who cannot feel an identification, in the parable of the two sons, with the reaction of the elder son who sees his wayward brother welcomed with love and joy by their father after he has squandered all his possessions (Luke 15.25–32)? Or with the workers who laboured the whole day long when they see their companions receive identical wages for a single hour of work (Matt 20.1–15)? A love without limits will always seem 'unfair' to our human condition, anxious to keep things on the level of merit so that we are able to remain in control.

But it is one thing to recognize in oneself vestiges of the 'old self' and thus the permanent need for conversion; it is quite another to make this attitude of refusal the basis of one's behaviour. In following the gospel story, we discover that this resistance to the newness of God by people who cling at all costs to their knowledge or their power is going to determine the ending of Jesus' life. By having him arrested and put to death by the Romans, his enemies think they have put an end to his work. The messenger is slain so that his message will be forgotten and those responsible for the deed can remain in charge, their power undisputed (cf. Luke 20.9–19). This way of thinking is evident, in any case, for those who follow the logic of 'might makes right'.

In the universe created by God, however, the only real one, things are not so simple. Far from being purely and simply a failure, the end of Jesus' earthly life will sum up the meaning of his entire existence and, in fact, of the whole history of salvation recounted in the Bible. Like the Israelites in the land of slavery or trapped on the banks of the Red Sea, like the exiles in Babylon, like so many victims of injustice down through the ages, Jesus is, humanly speaking, at a dead end, powerless and at the mercy of the forces of violence and death. But instead of reacting by employing the same weapons as his adversaries, he makes use of this horrible death to express his message even more profoundly. St John puts it most clearly:

Before the feast of Passover, Jesus, knowing that his hour had come, the hour to pass from this world to the Father, having loved his own in the world, loved them to the very end.

(John 13.1)

The sufferings and the death of Jesus become an occasion for him, by giving himself totally, to reveal the full extent of God's love (cf. John 15.13). In this way he shows the meaning of his life (Mark 10.45) and the identity of the One he calls 'Abba' (1 John 4.8–10). On the cross, all he has for his executioners are words of forgiveness (Luke 23.34; cf. 1 Pet 2.23).

And the confirmation that the cross is not the victory of violence and hatred, but in fact a revelation that a love that forgives is stronger than death, is given on the third day when the women come to the tomb and find it empty. The announcement of the resurrection is thus the Good News in a nutshell: it is significant that the spontaneous reaction of the women is to be 'utterly astonished' (Mark 16.5) or, in other versions, to set out immediately, full of joy, to share the news with others (Matt 28.8; cf. Luke 24.33 etc.). Everything that happened previously will now appear in a new light.

Questions for Reflection

1. In the parable of the Pharisee and the tax-collector (Luke 18.9–14), Jesus contrasts two attitudes towards God. Can we find these two attitudes in ourselves? If we assume that the prayer of both men was sincere, why was the Pharisee's prayer unacceptable? Why was the tax-collector, in spite of his wrongdoing, declared righteous by God?

2. How did Jesus reveal the meaning of his death on the cross by the two great signs he performed during his last meal with his disciples, washing their feet (John 13.1–17) and giving them bread and wine transformed into his body and blood (Luke 22.14–20)?

Explanatory Note

In the three synoptic gospels (Matt 12.22–32; Mark 3.22–30; Luke 11.14–23; 12.10), Jesus speaks of a 'blasphemy against the Holy Spirit' that will not be forgiven. To understand this obscure passage better, it is useful to distinguish three levels.

1. *In the life of Jesus recounted by Matthew*, this saying comes after Jesus cures a blind and dumb man possessed by an evil spirit. Motivated by jealousy, 'the Pharisees' (stereotyped adversaries of Jesus in Matthew's gospel) accuse him of casting out evil spirits through power given him by the ruler of these spirits.

Jesus responds to this grotesque accusation by saying, in effect, 'It is perhaps understandable that you are unable to recognize me as the One sent from God, the glorious Son of Man, since it is true that I have come to earth in an "unglorious" way to fulfil my mission, like the humble Servant predicted by the prophet Isaiah [cf. Matt 12.15–21]. But to consider the act of healing, of casting out evil and restoring the fullness of life, such a clear manifestation of God, as the work of the devil ... that is inexcusable. For that you have no need of a new revelation; it is enough to read and understand the Scriptures with which you pride yourselves on being so familiar.'

Why does Jesus describe this act as something that 'will not be forgiven'? Most probably we have here a reminiscence from the Old Testament. Exodus 23.20–23 speaks of an angel that God sends in front of his people to show them the way through the wilderness. God says 'Do not rebel against him, for he will not pardon your transgression'. Then in Exodus 33, Moses asks God not to send an angel, a sign that God is not satisfied with Israel, but to accompany the people himself (by 'his face'); God ultimately agrees to this request of Moses. Finally, Isaiah 63.7–14 goes a step further: it says clearly that 'it was no messenger or angel but his face that saved them' (v. 9). But God's 'face' (or 'presence', NRSV) is identified with his Spirit (vv. 11, 14) and Israel's unfaithfulness on the road is described in this way: 'they rebelled and grieved [or vexed, or saddened] his Holy Spirit' (v. 10; cf. Eph 4.30). Jesus' opponents are thus implicitly identified with their disbelieving ancestors during the Exodus: 'You have filled up the measure of your ancestors!' (Matt 23.32).

2. *At the time when the Gospel was written down, a generation later*, the text acquired a further dimension. In the eyes of the community for which Matthew is writing, the Pharisees criticized by Jesus are seen as typical of those who refuse to accept Jesus as the Messiah of Israel and who are in conflict with those who have become followers of Christ. Their 'blasphemy against the Spirit' is the refusal to recognize the Risen Christ present in his Church.

Luke, always concerned to distinguish the different stages of the story of salvation, puts the saying in another context. He follows it by a saying about the Holy Spirit who will defend the disciples during times of persecution (Luke 12.11–12). Luke thus implicitly contrasts Jesus' life on earth and those who rejected him then (cf. Acts 3.17: 'I know, my brothers, that you acted out of ignorance, along with your leaders') with the period after Pentecost when they no longer have any excuse (cf. Acts 13.46; 18.6; 28.25–28).

3. *What meaning can this saying have for us today?* First of all, it must not be separated from the Gospel message in its entirety, which tells of a God who loves the world to such an extent that he gives everything in order to share with it his own life (cf. John 3.16). There is no sin too great for God's forgiveness. God's forgiveness, in other words God's love, God's Spirit (cf. John 20.22–23) who renews us inwardly, is constantly offered to every person, for God who is love 'cannot deny himself' (2 Tim 2.13).

But this renewal of human beings is not automatic. What corresponds to it on the side of the receiver is conversion of heart, in other words our free choice to welcome into our existence an unconditional, unmerited love that transforms us. And God respects this free decision, for a love that imposed itself would be a logical contradiction. Expressed in positive terms, then, the saying underlines the great respect which God has for us; he never forces our freedom.

Human freedom thus implies the possibility of refusing to believe in God's love, to trust in the forgiveness he constantly offers. We know, by personal experience or by observation, that human beings can cling to a caricature of God (cf. Gen 3.4–5; Num 20.4–5), all the while realizing deep within themselves that it does not correspond to reality. Jesus wants to make us realize that God cannot directly overcome such a refusal as long as it persists. That is the 'weakness' of his love. But God does not withdraw his Spirit. The Good Shepherd keeps looking for ways to bring the lost sheep back to the fold. And it would be unjustified to draw from this saying the conclusion that there are *in fact* persons who have refused God's love to the very end: on the contrary, we are called to have hope for everyone.

In his encyclical letter *Dominum et Vivificantem* (no. 46), John Paul II writes, ' ... "blasphemy [against the Holy Spirit]" does not properly consist in offending against the Holy Spirit in words; it consists rather *in the refusal to accept the salvation which God offers to man through the Holy Spirit*, working through the power of the Cross ... [It] consists precisely in *the radical refusal to accept this forgiveness*, of which he is the intimate giver and which presupposes the genuine conversion which he brings about in the conscience ... This means the refusal to come to the sources of Redemption, which nevertheless remain "always" open ... The Spirit has infinite power to draw from these sources.'

IV

❧

A LIFE THAT OVERFLOWS

O F A L L the new things done by God since the world began, the resurrection of Christ is the summit. It is a mystery so overwhelming that it is difficult to speak about it in our present condition. Since the resurrection is the response, beyond all measure and all calculation, to the longing built by God into the structure and the history of the universe, all the different languages that human beings have forged to express this longing are brought to the peak of their intensity. It is like someone playing on an organ with all the stops pulled out; the danger is that our ears perceive only a cacophony.

Before attempting to listen to this concert in the pages of the New Testament, two remarks are in order. First of all, when we speak of Christ's resurrection, it is important to remember that it does not refer to a detached, individualistic event. When people today try to imagine the resurrection, they tend to think spontaneously of a corpse coming back to life, while the rest of the universe follows its preordained course as if nothing had happened. The Jewish contemporaries of Jesus, however, would have reacted in a quite different manner. For them, the very notion of resurrection implied a collective event, one that marked the end of an era and the beginning of a new age (cf. Dan 12.2–3). To proclaim that 'Christ is risen', then, was a way of affirming that the great turning-point of history had already taken place, that a process was underway that would last till the end of the world or, more precisely, that characterized the end (cf. 1 Cor 15.20–28).

In the second place, compared to the other 'marvels' accomplished by God in the course of history, beginning with the creation of the universe, Christ's resurrection is the one that offers the least access to our eyes of flesh. Everything has to be grasped from within the act of faith. Already at the time of the apostles, with the later exception of St Paul, the appearances of the Risen Christ were granted to the disciples alone. Seen from without there were only indirect or ambiguous signs, such as the empty tomb and — especially — the change which took place in believers. This explains a certain feeling, in approaching the proclamation of the resurrection, that something does not quite fit: there remains a persistent gap between the glorious descriptions of a new world and what is actually visible on the surface of human history.

Yet in spite of everything, the disciples of 'this Jesus, who was crucified' (cf. Acts 2.36) proclaimed unambiguously, full of joy and courage: 'He is risen!' Here we have in all probability the first formulation of the Good News on the lips of Christians. They saw in the event a demonstration of God's creative power (2 Cor 13.4), of the radiant energy of divine love (Rom 6.4): 'put to death in the flesh, he was made alive in the Spirit' (1 Pet 3.18b; cf. Rom 1.4). This total transformation of a human existence by a life stronger than death is the activity most characteristic of the Holy Spirit, as the prophet Ezekiel learned centuries earlier in his vision of the dry bones (Ezek 37.9–10).

In chapter 15 of his first letter to the Corinthians, St Paul speaks about the resurrection to Greeks, people to whom the very notion of a resurrected body would seem absurd. After using some images drawn from nature (1 Cor 15.35–44), the apostle bases his argument on the story of the creation of humanity found in the book of Genesis: 'Thus it is written: *the first man, Adam, became a living soul*; the last Adam, a life-giving spirit' (15.45). In other words, with the creation of the human body and soul, explained in Genesis 2.7, God's work was not completed; human beings were not yet fully what they were intended to be in God's eyes. It is only after the coming of Christ, or more precisely after his resurrection, that the work of creation enters its final stage. That is why Paul calls Christ 'the last Adam': he is the firstborn of a new humanity (cf. 1 Cor 15.20; Col 1.18; Rom 8.29; Rev 1.5).

In addition, Paul's comparison enables us to deepen our understanding of the global relationship between the old and the new in the Bible. Some Bible texts can give the impression that the new comes to take the place of the old, that it is a reality that replaces another reality of the same order. The mystery of the resurrection helps us understand that the new is rather a *transformation* or *transfiguration* of the old; its wounds are healed, its deviations corrected, and it is brought to an unhoped-for perfection. What is doomed to disappear are the elements that had only a provisional role to play, like the cocoon that protected the caterpillar or the covering of the seed (cf.

1 Cor 15.36, 42–44; John 12.24), like a temporary dwelling or clothes that have been outgrown (2 Cor 5.1–4).

Although St Paul refers to Christ as the second and last Adam, the man from heaven, this does not mean that in the apostle's eyes he is the founder of a new race of beings fated to replace humankind, as in a science-fiction novel. It is rather that through Christ, the descendants of the 'first Adam' are re-created; they become a new creation (2 Cor 5.17; Gal 6.15) which is at the same time the culmination of God's plan from the very beginning (Eph 1.4, 9–10). Once again, in God, always the same and always new, continuity and newness are not in opposition but are shown to be complementary.

Concretely, though, how did Christ accomplish his mission as the last Adam, the founder of a renewed humanity? In other words, what is the link between the Risen Lord and the other human beings who, through him, are meant to be born to a new life? In the text we have just examined, St Paul gives us the key:

the first man, Adam, became a living soul; the last Adam, *a life-giving spirit*.

(1 Cor 15.45)

One miracle is followed by another miracle of a different order. In Adam, God created a being capable of life and thought; the Risen Christ is someone infinitely greater, a being penetrated by the Creator Spirit of God to such an extent that he becomes a source of life for others, like a container so full of water that it overflows, or rather becomes a fountain that gushes forth (cf. John 4.14; 7.38).

This helps us to understand the close link found throughout the New Testament between the resurrection of Jesus and the gift of the Holy Spirit. If it is true that the meaning of the cross is incomprehensible unless we see it in the light of the resurrection, it is also true that, without the gift of the Holy Spirit, the Easter mystery would lack an essential element. We would not really see why it is true that Christ died 'for us' (cf. 1 Thess 5.10; Rom 5.8; 2 Cor 5.14–15), how the death and resurrection of 'someone else' can matter to me or change anything in my own life. Because they did not integrate fully the role of the Spirit, so many theologies of the past, particularly in the West, lost sight of the inner coherence of the Christian message. They were forced to fall back upon extrinsic notions like 'imitating' and 'following someone's example', or else to use images taken from the law court to try and account for the redemptive death of Christ. This did not help people's understanding of the Christian mystery: the Good News of new life was turned into a legalistic and dry moralism.

St John, always so careful to maintain the unity of the Easter mystery, shows this link between the resurrection and the gift of the Spirit already on the evening of Easter:

Jesus came and stood in their midst, and said to them, 'Peace be with you!' ... The disciples were overjoyed when they saw the Lord. So Jesus said to them again, 'Peace be with you! As the Father has sent me, so I am sending you.' When he had said this he breathed upon them and said to them, 'Receive the Holy Spirit ... '.

(John 20.19–22)

In a climate of joy and peace, the Risen Christ communicates to his disciples his breath, which is at the same time the Breath of God. This Breath of life is closely linked to their being sent into the world, as well as to the gift of forgiveness (John 20.23). Can we not perceive here a distant echo of the first creation, when God breathed the divine Breath of life into Adam before sending him into the garden to be responsible for the other creatures there (Gen 2.7–8)?

Questions for Reflection

1. Why did St Paul write to the Corinthians, 'If Christ is not risen, your faith is an illusion' (1 Cor 15.17)? What role does faith in the resurrection play in my life?

2. Read Luke 24.13–35. The disciples on the road to Emmaus know the entire history of Jesus up to and including the empty tomb and yet they are downcast (v. 17). Why? What does the Risen Christ do to enable them to see things in a new way? What does this story tell us about the way the Risen Lord is still present in the Christian community?

V

THE GIFT OF GOD

F A R   F R O M being the end of Jesus' career, his death on the cross is a passage, a Passover, towards the fullness of life. And this Passover is a new beginning, not just for Jesus but for the whole of God's creation. In other words, following its own logic, the Easter mystery culminates in a new sending forth of the Spirit to transfigure the face of the earth. Of all the gospel-writers, St Luke and St John are the ones who show most clearly the deep interconnections between these different aspects of the Easter mystery.

For his part, St John helps us to understand this link by means of the symbol of *water*, so frequent in his gospel. In chapter 4, Jesus meets a Samaritan woman next to a well. After asking her for something to drink, he speaks of some 'living water' that he is able to give, water that can fully quench her thirst and that will become in her 'a spring of water welling up to eternal life' (John 4.10–14). A little later in the gospel, during a holy-day celebration in Jerusalem, Jesus once again invites people to drink and he quotes the saying: 'Rivers of living water will flow from within him' (John 7.37–38). And the evangelist comments:

He said this about the Spirit that those who would believe in him were destined to receive; for the Spirit was not yet present, since Jesus had not yet been glorified.

(John 7.39)

We know, of course, that God's Spirit had been at work in the world from the very beginning. But here, Jesus is talking about the new and definitive coming of the Spirit to re-create the universe. In John's eyes, this will be the result of Jesus' glorification, in other words his death-and-resurrection, conceived of as a single reality.

Already at the time of Jesus' passion, St John shows us discreetly how this promise is fulfilled. At the moment of his death, we read, 'Jesus said, "It is accomplished" and, bowing his head, he handed over the spirit' (John 19.30). Where Mark's gospel has only a simple verb, whose root is the word for spirit ('he expired', Mark 15.37), Luke and Matthew accentuate Jesus' act of self-surrender into the Father's hands, one by quoting a psalm (Luke 23.46; Ps 31.5), the other by using a stronger verb ('he gave up the spirit', Matt 27.50). In neither case, however, is there a reference to the Holy Spirit; only Jesus' gift of his life is evoked. John though, in his inimitable fashion, turns the phrase into a play on words to express, once again, the unity of the paschal mystery: Jesus' death is at the same time the 'handing over' of the Holy Spirit, source of forgiveness and principle of a new creation.

Just in case this is not seen, a few verses further on the evangelist mentions a small detail to which he obviously attributes great importance:

... one of the soldiers pierced his side with a lance, and immediately blood and water came out. The person who saw this has testified to it, and his testimony is trustworthy, and that one knows that he speaks truly, so that you too might believe.

(John 19.34–35)

Why this insistence? The fact in itself, even if it is unusual, does not seem to warrant it. But if we recall the significance of water in this gospel, we are led to seek the symbolic meaning of the event: in his death, or more precisely by the gift of his life (signified here by the blood), Jesus becomes for us a spring of living water, in other words he communicates the Spirit.*

If John is without equal in affirming the unity of the paschal mystery, the close interrelationship between Christ's death and resurrection and the gift of the Spirit, St Luke, with his historian's outlook, shows most clearly the culmination of this mystery in a new stage in the history of salvation, characterized by the pouring out of the Holy Spirit 'upon all flesh'. To do this, Luke is obliged to write a second book, the Acts of the Apostles, for in his eyes the gospel would have been incomplete had it ended with Jesus' resurrection without showing the universal significance of that event.

At the end of his gospel, Luke already prepares us

---

*On another level, some have seen in this symbolism an allusion to baptism (cf. John 3.5) and the Eucharist (cf. John 6.53–56). Perhaps for this reason the first letter of John can say that the water and the blood continue to bear witness in the life of the Church (1 John 5.7–8). But in the dynamic of the fourth gospel, this dimension remains secondary.

for the new stage to come. The Risen Christ says to his disciples:

And look, I am going to send upon you what my Father has promised. As for you, remain in the city until you are clothed with power from on high.

(Luke 24.49)

Everything remains in suspense, oriented towards a future fulfilment. And when Jesus goes up to heaven while blessing them, a 'great joy' (cf. Luke 2.10) fills the disciples and a current of praise begins to flow between heaven and earth (Luke 24.50–53). These are clear indications that we are not witnessing an absence but a new form of presence.

At the beginning of the second volume of Luke's work, the Risen Lord uses the same terms — 'what the Father has promised' (Acts 1.4), 'power' (*dynamis*, 1.8) — and he explains:

John baptized with water, but you are going to be baptized with the Holy Spirit a few days from now.

(Acts 1.5)

The Baptist's words (Luke 3.16–17), a summing up of the entire prophetic tradition, are now about to find their fulfilment. The great and definitive outpouring of the Lord's Spirit is going to transform the world, flooding it with the eternal Newness of God.

And so we come to the day of Pentecost. Before becoming a Christian feast, Pentecost, fifty days after Passover, was — and still is — a Jewish holy day. One of the three high holy days of the year (Exod 23.14–17), called the Festival of Harvest or of Weeks (Shavuoth), it commemorates the event of Sinai (Exod 19), the formation of God's people through the gift of the Torah. It is thus the memorial of the covenant between Israel and its God. But that year in Jerusalem, Pentecost would not be a simple re-enactment of the past, but an authentic new beginning. To understand this, we need to return to the vision of the great prophets of Israel.

The Bible shows clearly that the history of God's people is far from being a model of perfection. More often than not, the nation did not follow the way of the Lord in an attitude of trust expressed by the readiness to live according to God's will. For this reason, prophets arose to call people to repent and return to God, generally without much apparent success. Jeremiah, for instance, suffered deeply on account of the apostasy of his contemporaries and his inability to do anything about it. At the same time, he believed firmly that the Lord would never abandon his wayward people and would find a way beyond all human logic to touch their heart. This marriage of lucidity and hope, so characteristic of the great prophets, was the soil from which sprang the following oracle, one of the high-water marks of the biblical faith:

The days are surely coming, says the Lord, when I will make a new covenant with the house of Israel and the house of Judah. It will not be like the covenant that I made with their ancestors when I took them by the hand to bring them out of the land of Egypt — a covenant that they broke, though I was their husband, says the Lord. But this is the covenant that I will make with the house of Israel after those days, says the Lord: I will put my law within them, and I will write it on their hearts; and I will be their God, and they shall be my people. No longer shall they teach one another, or say to each other, 'Know the Lord', for they shall all know me, from the least of them to the greatest, says the Lord, for I will forgive their iniquity, and remember their sin no more.

(Jer 31.31–34)

If human beings are unable to have an authentic relationship with the Lord, in Jeremiah's eyes there is only one solution: God must take the initiative and transform the heart of his partner. This will be an act of divine mercy that will bring about an interiorization of the Torah; from now on, those whose hearts have been thus transformed will know the will of the Lord from within and will therefore live in unbroken intimacy with God.

It is worth pointing out that, here too, the word 'new' does not refer to a second reality which comes to replace a prior reality of the same order. God has no intention of creating another race of beings, and the prophet is far from imagining that God is going to forsake Israel in favour of another nation. The 'new covenant' is rather the perfect interiorization of the already existing covenant by the human partner, henceforth capable of a perfect fidelity to God.

This inspired intuition of Jeremiah was taken up and made more explicit by others after him. A generation later, the prophet Ezekiel tells us more about the way in which God will accomplish this transformation:

I will sprinkle clean water upon you, and you shall be clean from all your uncleannesses, and from all your idols I will cleanse you. A new heart I will give you, and a new spirit I will put within you; and I will remove from your body the heart of stone and give you a heart of flesh. I will put my spirit within you, and make you follow my statutes and be careful to observe my ordinances.

(Ezek 36.25–27)

God's forgiveness will bring about a total transformation of the human heart by the presence of the Holy Spirit who will henceforth dwell there. The prophet Joel, in his turn, announces an outpouring of the Spirit on all flesh (Joel 2.28–29), and a mysterious prophecy in the book of Zechariah speaks of 'a spirit of compassion and supplication' which God pours out, leading to the people's return to God and a fountain of water that springs up for the forgiveness of their sins (Zech 12.10 – 13.1). Outpouring of the Holy Spirit, forgiveness, water, the covenant renewed: this cluster of images and concepts keeps on appearing in the prophetic books in order to indicate a hope.

According to the Christian faith, it is around Jesus Christ that all of these fragments finally coalesce into a coherent whole. In the wake of Jesus' Passover, the first Pentecost (Acts 2) is not simply a celebration of the Sinai covenant made present once again through worship; it is the moment of the revelation of the covenant completely renewed by Christ's gift of his life. The apostles' house is filled with wind and fire, evoking the storm on Mount Sinai (Exod 19.16–18); but this is above all a tangible sign of the presence of the Holy Spirit. For this time, God does not write his Law on tablets of stone but on the hearts of the apostles, by 'tongues as of fire' (Acts 2.3) which represent the gift of the Holy Spirit.

Then Peter begins to speak (once again, Spirit and word are inseparably joined) in order to explain to the crowd the meaning of what has happened. He quotes the prophecy of Joel that speaks of the Day of the Lord, characterized by the outpouring of the Spirit on 'all flesh'. And he tells his hearers that this prophecy is now coming true (Acts 2.16, 33). This can easily give rise to a question: how can this prophecy concerning the transformation of the entire nation, and even the entire universe (Acts 2.17–20 = Joel 2.28–31), be fulfilled by an event which only involves a small group of people? Is Peter's explanation simply an exaggeration 'for the good of the cause'?

The answer to this question is of great importance for understanding the logic of the new covenant. Here we are not dealing with an exaggeration, but with a *recapitulation* or *anticipation*. In other words, to make a completely new start for the human race, God does not change everything everywhere all at once, as if by magic. Instead the new reality first appears fully formed 'in miniature', and from that point in time and space it begins to radiate outwards. The event in Jerusalem is only a beginning, or rather a seed, like the mustard seed that Jesus referred to in his teaching (Matt 13.31–32). Now, those who receive the Spirit have to find ways of communicating it to others. A vast movement of universal scope has been set in motion.

Questions for Reflection

1. As opposed to the gospels of Luke and John, Matthew's gospel does not relate the resurrection of Jesus to the gift of the Spirit. How does Matthew, in the appearance of the Risen Christ recounted at the end of his gospel (Matt 28.16–20), nonetheless express the same concerns that the other evangelists do when they speak of the Spirit?

2. During his meeting with the Samaritan woman

(John 4.1–15), Jesus first asks for something to drink and then offers to give her something. Why? Do I see God primarily as someone who makes demands or as someone who gives? What can we do to receive living water from Christ?

3. When the disciples ask the Risen Christ to reveal to them the day when his Kingdom will be inaugurated (Acts 1.6–8), what is the meaning of his seemingly negative reply? To what extent does he in fact address their concern?

VI

BORN OF THE SPIRIT

THE SPIRIT, definitively liberated by Christ through the gift of his life on the cross, is now able to flood the universe with the dynamism of a vivifying and transforming presence. But this transformation does not take place instantaneously nor in a dis-ordered fashion. It follows its own logic, submitting to the needs of the world created by God. It shows its fruits first of all in the resurrection of Christ himself, who thus becomes 'the firstborn of many brothers and sisters' (Rom 8.29), then in the transformation of a small group of disciples who become 'witnesses' (Acts 1.8) to this Life stronger than death.

What happens in Jerusalem on Pentecost day is thus the starting point of an upheaval that sends out its shock waves 'to the ends of the earth' (Acts 1.8). And so Peter, after having made the connection between the gift of the Spirit and the life, death and resurrection of 'Jesus the Nazorean', concludes his speech with these words:

Change your hearts, and let each of you be baptized in the name of Jesus Christ for the forgiveness of your sins, and you will receive the gift of the Holy Spirit. For the promise is for you and for your children, as well as for all those who are far away ...

(Acts 2.38–39)

For John, the rite of baptism was a sign of repentance in order to prepare oneself for the new age to come. And now it becomes, for Christians, the expression of an ongoing Pentecost. By saying yes to Christ, the baptized open their heart to receive the Spirit who brings forgiveness; they welcome the love of God which makes them a new being.

Later on in the book of Acts, proclaiming in his turn the faith of the apostles, Paul describes the resurrection of Jesus using another image drawn from a psalm. Psalm 2 celebrates the enthronement of the king, officially recognized by God as his Son:

And we announce to you the Good News: the promise made to our ancestors that God brought to final fulfilment for us, their descendants, by raising up Jesus, as it is also written in the second psalm: You are my son; today I have begotten you.

(Acts 13.32–33)

St Luke had used this same verse (Ps 2.7) in his account of the baptism of Jesus and the descent of the Holy Spirit upon him (Luke 3.22). It has generally been seen as a justification of the messianic title 'Son of God', definitively bequeathed to Jesus by his resurrection from the dead and already prefigured at the beginning of his ministry. But something else is worthy of interest here: by means of this quotation, the activity of God who, by his Spirit, does a new thing is implicitly described as a begetting, a bringing to birth. Christ's resurrection, prefigured by his baptism, is a new birth, resulting from the direct intervention of the Spirit of God (cf. Rom 8.29; Col 1.15; Rev 1.5).

It is noteworthy in this regard to recall that the image of birth was used very early by Christians as a preferred way of referring to their baptism. Already, in the gospel of John, Jesus had explained to Nicodemus that, without a new birth from above, in other words from God (cf. John 1.13), a birth 'of water and of Spirit', no one can enter the Kingdom of God (John 3.1–8). And Jesus attempted to make Nicodemus, who remained attached to the literal meaning of the words, understand that he did not have to repeat a second time what had already taken place, but to let what already existed be transfigured by the creative Breath of God.

Similarly, speaking of baptism, St Paul wrote to Titus, 'because of his mercy, [God] saved us by means of the bath of new birth and renewal in the Holy Spirit' (Tit 3.5). St Peter, in turn, reminds the newly baptized: 'You have been begotten anew by a seed that is not perishable but imperishable, through the living and lasting Word of God' (1 Pet 1.23). And St James: 'By his own will, [the Father] brought us to birth by the word of truth, so that we might be a kind of first fruits of his creatures' (James 1.18). The entry into the Christian life seen as a new birth is part of the common patrimony of the early Christians. But far from being a simple metaphor to express a sociological transition, the expression has to be understood in a strong and profound sense. By his resurrection, Christ is born to a new life and thus inaugurates definitively a new creation into which we are able to enter. In other words, God's Spirit is henceforth fully at home in our human world, accomplishing a new Pentecost to which we have access by our baptism.

The baptized person enters a new life which is 'eternal' (Rom 6.23; 1 John 5.13 etc.). This word does not refer primarily to the duration of the life but above all to its *quality*: it is the life of resurrection, the very life of God that penetrates and transfigures human existence. Whoever enters this life is transformed down to the very depths of their self. They receive a new identity, in biblical terms a new name. The book of Revelation shows us the fulfilment of this promise, made centuries earlier (Isa 62.2; 65.15):

To the victor I will give ... a white stone with a new name written on it, known to nobody but the one who receives it.
(Rev 2.17)

At the same time, what is begun and summed up in our baptism has to unfold until it penetrates and transforms the whole of our existence. Here we are once again following the logic of the new covenant: everything is given, but in embryo, as a life-principle called to undergo a long process of development. If we died in order to be reborn with Christ in baptism, writes St Paul to the Romans, that is so that we can start living a new life (Rom 6.4). Similarly, St John affirms that those who are 'born of God' can be recognized by the fact that they are no longer attracted by sin (1 John 3.9; 5.18); on the contrary, they 'walk in the light' (1 John 1.7) by loving their brothers and sisters (1 John 4.7), by doing what is right (1 John 2.29; 3.10). For the presence of the Spirit in us causes a kind of permanent process of birth:

... even if our outer self is wasting away, our inner self is being renewed day by day.
(2 Cor 4.16)

Questions for Reflection

1. The New Testament presents baptism not just as the beginning of the Christian life but as its recapitulation. How do we live out the following aspects of baptism in the course of our life as believers: *metanoia* (conversion, change of heart, Acts 2.38); passing with Christ from death to life (Rom 6.4; Col 2.12); welcoming God's forgiveness (Acts 2.38; 22.16); trusting in Christ by trusting his disciples as well (Acts 8.12–13; 18.8)?

2. All the different ways we say 'yes' to Christ our whole life long are not added to the 'yes' of baptism; they are that same 'yes' taken up again and applied to a specific situation. How am I called to say this 'yes' of my baptism by specific decisions for the sake of Christ and the Gospel (choice of studies, of work, temporary commitments ...)? How can I live out the 'yes' of baptism by a lifelong commitment (marriage, ordained ministry, community life ...)?

PART THREE

THE NEW HAS COME
(2 Corinthians 5.17)

I

SIGNS OF LIFE

THE CHRISTIAN life is thus not, in essence, just another philosophy or even a new religion but the entry into a new creation (cf. Gal 6.15). The cross of Christ opened the floodgates to a new and definitive outpouring of the Creator Spirit, first to animate and transfigure the humanity of the Son of God (Easter), then to incorporate us into that renewed humanity (Pentecost). By welcoming the Good News and by responding by faith expressed in the yes of baptism, believers enter into a new relationship with God (a new covenant), receive a new identity (a new name), begin a new life that is constantly being renewed. The God of the Bible, whose hallmark is the ability to create something new, thus lays bare the depths of his being in the Passover of his only Son.

And now a question arises: what enables us to recognize this new creation taking place in and around us? We have already seen that, for the Bible, the Spirit lies at the opposite extreme from a pure abstraction. Since the Spirit is, on the contrary, the source of dynamism of life itself, its presence must of necessity be manifested by tangible *signs*. We are thus justified in asking: what are the signs of this new life brought into being by Christ? This question is essential, if faith is not to be reduced to an illusion or a mere utopia.

According to the New Testament as a whole, there is one great sign of this new reality, expressed by each author in his own way and giving rise to a multitude of secondary signs. This great sign can already be glimpsed in the account of the first Christian Pentecost: 'devout Jews from all the nations under heaven' hear the apostles speaking, each of them in their own tongue (Acts 2.5–12). The first manifestation of the gift of the Spirit is a miracle of communication. While maintaining the diversity ('each in his own tongue'), the Spirit is the source of a new unity among human beings; the curse of Babel (Gen 11) is finally lifted.

What is expressed here in symbolic fashion immediately begins to take on concrete form. After Peter's explanation to the crowd, we read:

Those who accepted his teaching were baptized, and that day about three thousand people were added to their number. They were devoted to the apostles' teaching and the fellowship, to the breaking of the bread and the prayers. Everyone was overawed — many wonders and signs came about through the apostles. All the believers were united and shared everything in common, selling their property and possessions and sharing the proceeds with all, to each according to their needs. They met together faithfully each day in the Temple, and celebrated the breaking of the bread in their homes, sharing meals joyfully and in simplicity of heart, praising God and enjoying a good reputation among the whole people. And the Lord added to their community day by day those who were finding salvation.

(Acts 2.41–46; cf. 4.32–35; 5.12–16)

Chapter 2 of the Acts of the Apostles culminates in the description of a *community*, a community of prayer and sharing, in constant expansion. In this community, the gathering of all nations announced by the prophets (Isa 2.1–4; 60; Zech 8.20–23; etc.) and prefigured on Pentecost morning is already lived out in a microcosm. By its existence, this community bears witness to the fact that the Gospel is not a utopia but an ongoing new creation.

The name often given by the New Testament to this new community, born of Christ's death and resurrection and the outpouring of his Spirit, is the word *ekklēsia*, usually translated into English by 'church' but literally meaning 'assembly, congregation'. This expression had already been employed, in the Greek translation of the Hebrew Scriptures, to translate the Hebrew word *qahal*, when it referred to the gathering of the entire holy people called together by God in the wilderness (Acts 7.38; Deut 9.10; 18.16; cf. 4.10; 23.2–9). On the lips of Christians, it soon became a expression used to refer to the community of the baptized, either in one place (e.g. 1 Cor 1.2: 'the Church of God which is in Corinth') or on a universal scale (e.g. Gal 1.13; Eph 1.22–23). To understand the manner in which the New Testament speaks of the Church, we must constantly keep in mind its fundamental significance for believers: while viewing itself as in historical continuity with God's people formed by the covenant on Sinai, it is at the same time a fulfilment, a new creation. This *ekklēsia* of the 'final days' (Heb 1.2) is the starting point of the universal ingathering of the whole of humanity by Christ and the Holy Spirit.

At the same time, it would be false to attribute to

the New Testament writers a naively idealistic outlook. St Luke celebrates, it is true, the existence of a community of prayer and sharing which 'enjoyed a good reputation among the whole people' (Acts 2.47; cf. 4.33; 5.13), but he does not underplay the difficulties both within the community and with those on the outside. Likewise, most of the letters found in the New Testament are written for the purpose of calling Christians to be faithful to their identity, which obviously means they are not yet fully what they should be.

If the Church in the New Testament, as the community of those reconciled by Christ, is a concrete reality subject to all the hazards of the human condition, it is also something extremely dynamic. When we read, in the Acts of the Apostles, that 'believers in ever greater numbers joined the Lord — whole crowds of men and women' (Acts 5.14; cf. 11.24), we realize that the boundaries between 'Church' and 'world' have not been drawn once and for all. The first Christians saw with their own eyes the tiny seed becoming a magnificent plant, the yeast causing the dough of all humanity to rise (cf. Matt 13.31–33). The Church appeared to them as a new humanity in the process of becoming, a new creation beginning to blossom in many different places. It was a springtime in flower.

Questions for Reflection

1. Are our local churches communities of prayer and sharing such as those described in the Acts of the Apostles (Acts 2.42–46; 4.32–35; 5.12–16)? While remembering that, even at the beginning, the Church

never lived out its identity to the full (see e.g. Acts 5.1ff.; 6.1), what can we do to make progress in this direction?

2. The name 'church'(*ekklēsia, qahal*) emphasizes the fact that what gathers us together in community is not a human initiative but a call from God, a divine act. What consequences does this truth have for the understanding of our identity as Christians?

3. On Pentecost day, people from 'every nation' heard, each in their own tongue, the apostles proclaim the saving works of God. What can we do, beginning on a local level, so that our churches can speak the language of every human being? How can we find room in our churches for the values of every culture and nation?

II

———— ❧ ————

PAUL: A DOUBLE
RECONCILIATION

ACCORDING TO the Acts of the Apostles, the great
sign or sacrament that bears witness to the appearance of the new covenant is the existence of a
universal community in a process of constant growth.
Let us now look at how the other New Testament
writers, especially Paul and John, express in their
turn this essential reality.

To gain a deeper understanding of St Paul's thinking on this subject, we can begin with this important
text:

Anyone who is in Christ is part of a new creation: the old
order has passed away, and something new has come into
being. This is all the work of God, who has reconciled us to
himself through Christ and has given us the ministry of
reconciliation. What I mean is this: God was in Christ
reconciling the world to himself, not counting people's
transgressions against them, and placing in us the message
of reconciliation. So we are ambassadors of Christ; through
us God is, as it were, making an appeal. In Christ's name
we beg you, be reconciled to God!

(2 Cor 5.17–20)

St Paul describes the new creation as fundamentally a
reconciliation: where once there was enmity between
human beings and God, there is now a new relationship. God is not the one who had broken off contacts

with us: Paul never says 'God has reconciled himself with us'. In his thinking, the break came from the side of human beings. And now, through Christ, God has made peace by an utterly free act of forgiveness. Free, but none the less concrete: by sending his Son, 'born of a woman and born under the Law' (Gal 4.4), God so to speak closed the gap from the human side. As a result, all we are required to do is to enter into the new situation created by God and proclaimed by those who have already experienced it, those who have in consequence received the ministry of communicating it to others.

The starting point of the new creation is thus a reconciliation between God and human beings. Nevertheless, when this is achieved an important dimension is still missing. For Paul, the ineluctable consequence of this reconciliation with God is a reconciliation among human beings. Writing to the Galatians, he begins by expressing the new relationship with God by means of two related images:

You are all sons of God through faith in Christ Jesus. All of you who were baptized into Christ have been clothed in Christ.

(Gal 3.26–27)

The first image is taken from the field of family relations. The act of reconciliation accomplished by God makes us members of God's own family. It is true that this image has lost much of its impact in a civilization where the family is rapidly losing its importance, its identity, and even its existence. For Paul and his contemporaries, however, being a son or daughter of God meant being situated within a reality that encompassed most of life's concerns, an overarching context that gave meaning and security to the whole of one's existence. It meant that one was no longer 'on the outside' ('strangers', Eph 2.19) or in a subordinate position ('slaves', Gal 4.7), but full members enjoying all the rights of membership.

But if the image of the family still remains comprehensible in spite of everything, the same thing is not true for the other image in this passage, that of 'being clothed in Christ'. In the contemporary Western world, we have become accustomed to a kind of anarchy with respect to clothing. The clothes we wear generally reflect only an individual, often idiosyncratic 'taste'. In the ancient world, however, the clothing worn was an unmistakable sign of one's personal *identity*, of one's place in society (one's sex, social class, occupation, nationality etc.). Saying that, through baptism, we have put on Christ, was therefore equivalent to saying that we have received a new identity, that of Christ himself, and that as a result God relates to us in exactly the same way that he relates to his Son. Then Paul goes further:

There is no 'Jew or Greek', there is no 'slave or free', there is no 'male and female'; for you are all one in Christ Jesus.

(Gal 3.28)

Because of this new identity, all the former identities, so important in the eyes of the world, have become relative. Naturally Paul is not unaware that, in the Christian community just as in the wider society, these distinctions still existed. Nor is he arguing here that all differences should be abolished. He is not concerned with uniformity but with reconciliation: the differences between people, whatever may be their relative justification on other levels, must not damage that fundamental unity in Christ which makes us 'Abraham's offspring' (Gal 3.16, 29). In God's family, diversity exists for the sake of communion, for division would radically contradict the Christian calling (cf. 1 Cor 1.13a).

The letter to the Colossians takes up the image of the old clothes that are taken off in order to put on new ones, linked to reconciliation among human beings:

> You have taken off the old self with its practices and put on the new self, the one that constantly renews itself in knowledge in the image of its creator, where there is no 'Greek and Jew', no 'circumcised and uncircumcised', no barbarian, Scythian, slave, free citizen — just Christ, who is all and who is in all.

> (Col 3.9b–11)

Here, the new humanity is characterized by a constant process of renewal, a process by which it becomes more and more like Christ, its Head and its starting point, who is the image of God (Col 1.15–18). Once again, unity with God through Christ necessarily implies unity among human beings.

In the following verses (Col 3.12ff.), the author takes up the question 'how can this unity come about?' In his eyes, of course, the transition from the 'old self' to the 'new self' is essentially the work of God (cf. Col 1.21–22; 2.11ff.); left to ourselves we would be unable to accomplish it. And yet this fact in no way justifies an attitude of passivity, for it is up to us to put into practice, by the way we live, what we have received as a gift. We do this by a life of kindness and of mutual forgiveness, in other words by a life of love (Col

3.12–14). The end result of all this is that 'the peace of Christ' will radiate outwards through the witness of men and women 'called in one body' (Col 3.15).

Among all the Pauline writings, the most coherent vision of this double reconciliation is surely to be found in the letter to the Ephesians. Writing to Christians of non-Jewish background (here referred to as 'Greeks'), the author sees the division between Jews and non-Jews as the paramount human division and thus the one capable of standing for all the others. So he writes:

[Christ] is our peace; he made the two one and broke down the wall of division separating them, the hostility, in his own flesh ... in order to create out of the two in himself one new humanity, making peace, and to reconcile both to God in one body through the cross; there, he put their hostility to death ... Through him, we both have free access in one Spirit to the Father.

(Eph 2.14–18)

Here the paschal mystery, on the one hand, and reconciliation with God and among human beings, on the other, are viewed in their basic unity. The new humanity* 'created according to God' (Eph 4.24) is the crucified and risen Christ; it is likewise the community born of the gift of Jesus' life. Christ's body is both that which hung on the cross and the Body of

---

*I have preferred to translate here the expression *kainos anthrōpos* in this way, in order to bring out the different levels superimposed in the apostle's thought. He does not consider Christ only as an individual, but as the 'last Adam', founder and recapitulation ('Head') of a new humanity. The translations 'new man' or 'new self' do not bring out as clearly this second level.

Christ which is the congregation of the faithful (cf. Eph 1.23; 5.30).

From these texts it is clear that, for St Paul, the pre-eminent sign of the ongoing new creation is the existence of communities where human beings from different backgrounds come together in the unity of love, where the divisions that habitually separate them are abolished. It should be emphasized again that, for Paul as well as for the other New Testament writers, there was nothing theoretical about this. During the exercise of their apostolic ministry, they saw with their own eyes men and women from the most varied cultures and outlooks begin to call each other brothers and sisters, and live together like members of the same family. This was assuredly something new in the history of the human race: for the first time, the notion of a single 'human family' appeared not only desirable in theory, but capable of being realized in practice.

St Paul sees the existence of this reconciled community as essentially the result of God's work, but he also knows that it cannot exist without the active collaboration of believers. His letters, therefore, generally contain one section where he explains the Father's plan accomplished by the Son and the Holy Spirit and another section where he exhorts his readers to collaborate with what God is doing:

I urge you, my brothers and sisters, in the name of our Lord Jesus Christ, to agree among yourselves; let there be no divisions among you; be fully united in mind and in purpose. (...) Make me perfectly happy by being fully in harmony, united in love and in spirit. Strive to be one; do nothing out of selfishness ...

(1 Cor 1.10; Phil 2.2–3a)

Become more and more what you are in reality, St Paul says in effect, for our faith is both a gift and a call to action, a responsibility.

In many cases, the problems which arise in the community are an occasion for the apostle to help the faithful to deepen their understanding of the Gospel. This was the situation notably in Corinth, a boisterous city where the community of believers was exposed to all sorts of trends and influences, which rendered their unity precarious. Among other things, a difference of opinion arose regarding the gifts of the Spirit. Some were attracted by the more spectacular gifts, such as speaking in tongues, and this led to rivalries and to discord.

In chapters 12 to 14 of his first letter to the Corinthians, St Paul tries to point the way to a solution of this problem. He explains to the community that all of the gifts, in their great diversity, have a common source: they come from the same God, the same Christ, the same Spirit (1 Cor 12.4–11). This unique origin is by no means an accident, for it corresponds to the purpose of the gifts. God sent the Spirit to reconcile us, so that, in Christ, we might form one Body:

For we were all baptized in one Spirit into one Body, whether Jew or Greek, whether slave or free, and we were all given of one Spirit to drink.

(1 Cor 12.13)

It is therefore meaningless to speak of more important and less important gifts, as if it were a question of privileges or honours to exalt one's personal identity or to prop up one's self-esteem. On the contrary, these gifts were all granted 'for the common good' (1

Cor 12.7), to 'build up' the community (1 Cor 14.5, 12, 26). It follows that the 'best' gifts, if one can put it that way, are those which help others the most, those which reinforce the unity of the body as a whole. The Holy Spirit's presence is not a source of anarchy and confusion; it is recognized by the harmony it makes possible.

That is why, in the midst of the practical advice he gives concerning different gifts and ministries, Paul stops to include a magnificent hymn to *agapē*, to charity or Christian love (1 Cor 13). For Paul, love is not just one gift among others, but 'a way that exceeds them all' (1 Cor 12.31). The various gifts are simply means to build up the community, whereas love is the expression of communion itself, the essence of community. For this reason, without love even the most spectacular gifts no longer have any reason for being; they can even play a negative role by becoming factors of division. Once again we see that, for St Paul, the presence of the Holy Spirit, source of an ongoing new creation, is made manifest by the existence of a community that tries to live out reconciliation day by day. The 'new life' in Christ is that of women and men who 'walk along the road of love, just as Christ loved us and offered himself to God for us' (Eph 5.2).

Questions for Reflection

1. How can we be 'ambassadors of reconciliation' (cf. 2 Cor 5.20), in other words how can we communicate, by our lives as much as by our words, the image of a God who is always ready to forgive?
2. Where is there a need for reconciliation around me

— in my personal life, in the Church, in society, in the world? What can I do to open these situations to the transforming dynamism of the Spirit?

3. How can we be attentive to the gifts of others, so that differences do not lead to division but to a life-giving diversity? Why does St Paul encourage believers to 'view others as better than themselves' (Phil 2.3)?

III

❧

JOHN: THE NEW
COMMANDMENT

DESPITE THEIR differences in approach and in
the language they use, St John and St Paul are one in
their vision of the main sign of the new reality
brought by Jesus Christ. In the last conversation he
has with his disciples before his death, presented by
John as a kind of last will and testament, Jesus speaks
these words:

> I give you a new commandment:
> love one another.
> As I have loved you,
> so must you love one another.
>
> (John 13.34)

We may wonder just what is new about this commandment. Did not the Torah already say quite
clearly: 'You shall love your neighbour as yourself'
(Lev 19.18)? The newness is indicated by these
words of Christ: love *as I have loved you*. The word
'as' (*kathōs*) means much more than just an outward
similarity between two beings or objects; it implies a
causal link. For St John, we can put into practice the
commandment of mutual love only because, first of
all, Jesus loved us to the point of giving his life for us
(cf. 1 John 4.9–11). Because of this gift of his life, we
can and must love, in other words give our lives in

turn (1 John 3.16; 4.11). In this way, the love of God in us reaches its goal, comes to its full flowering (1 John 4.12; 2.5). In a certain sense, then, love is not basically an activity that we perform; it is rather God who loves through us, by making use of our active collaboration.

Put another way, what is new about the Gospel is that the command to love is not in essence an order that comes from without, a precept written in a book or commanded by an authority who does not provide the means to put it into practice. Instead, this commandment is a concrete reality manifested in God's love present in the life of Jesus, and in us in our turn. In short, the commandment is new because it is the commandment of the new covenant, henceforth written not on stone tablets but on the hearts of the faithful.

And Jesus continues:

> In this way all will know that you are my disciples:
> if you have love for one another.
>
> (John 13.35)

Jesus tells us here that the sign of this new covenant is the existence of a space in the midst of the world where the commandment of love can be lived out concretely and reciprocally, day after day. We see this more clearly a little later in John's gospel, when Jesus explains in another way how the disciples will bear witness to him:

> ... that they all may be one,
> as you, Father, are in me and I in you;
> that they too may be in us,
> so that the world may believe that you sent me.

> ... that they may be one as we are one —
> I in them and you in me —
> that they may be made perfect in oneness,
> so that the world may know that you sent me
> and that you loved them as you loved me.
>
> (John 17.21–23)

By replacing the verb 'to love' with the expression 'to be one', Jesus helps us understand that the love he is speaking about is neither a simple feeling nor a unilateral act of kindness. Jesus is talking about the creation of new human relationships, of life shared over a period of time, in short, of a life of community, of communion. That is why the Johannine writings speak only of love between believers ('brothers and sisters', 'one another'), whereas Matthew and Luke mention love of enemies: this is in no way an attempt to restrict love to those who are 'like us' — the Christian community remains open to all — but because, in John's eyes, one cannot speak of true, 'perfected' love (1 John 4.12; 2.5) unless there is reciprocity, in other words where this love brings to birth a common life. This common life, the expression of mutual love, is the reality that becomes a sign for the world.

It is significant that, in these chapters of St John's gospel, Jesus refers several times to the Holy Spirit (John 14.15–17, 26; 15.26; 16.7–15). This insistence is in harmony with the message of the New Testament as a whole, which underlines the role of the Spirit in bringing about the new creation in Christ. But in this part of his gospel, John does not use images that describe the Spirit as a simple dynamism, a source of life (fire, water, wind ...). He emphasizes here the *personal* dimension of the Spirit; since nothing in God is impersonal, this 'force' or 'energy' is at the same time a person.

Thus the fourth gospel offers us the most developed teaching concerning the Spirit to be found in the entire New Testament. A teaching that at first may appear somewhat disconcerting, because it does not consider the Spirit primarily as the source of new life (but see John 3.5) or of love. The Spirit is the one who replaces Jesus as *Paraclete*, a word whose primary meaning is the advocate who defends the accused person in court. The Spirit's role is to keep the truth of the Gospel alive in Christ's disciples. He is a *witness* to the identity of Jesus who will transform the disciples into witnesses (John 15.26–27). He will ensure that the world's arguments against Jesus and his followers are shown to be groundless (John 16.8–11). Here we are in the realm of legal images; the Holy Spirit is the defence counsel who takes the side of believers in the great trial that opposes the world and God (cf. Matt 10.19–20).

But the Paraclete defends and supports the disciples above all by being a personal and inward source of knowledge, a *teacher*. He does not add anything to Christ's teaching, but causes it to penetrate the disciples' hearts and remain a living reality within them (John 14.26; 16.13; 1 John 2.20, 27). This is the angle from which John shows the relationship between the Spirit and new life. The Spirit's presence ensures that Christ's words never become a dead letter, but that they take root and bear fruit in the heart and the life of his followers. In this way, through the Holy Spirit, the Good News takes on flesh in the existence of each one of us, thus fulfilling the great prophecies of Jeremiah and Ezekiel when they spoke about the new covenant.

Questions for Reflection

1. In the introduction to his first letter (1 John 1.1–4), St John describes the purpose of the transmission of the Good News with the word *koinōnia*, communion or fellowship. How does this notion sum up the teaching of Jesus in his final conversation with his disciples (John 13 – 17)?

2. Why is the world which is hostile to God unable to recognize the Spirit (John 14.17)? What does this tell us about the way God acts towards creation? Why does Jesus insist that the Paraclete does not have a message of his own (John 16.13–15)? To what extent does this provide us with a principle to help in the discernment of spirits?

IV

FREE TO LOVE

FOR THE New Testament as a whole, the principal sign of the new creation undertaken by God through Christ and the Holy Spirit is the presence, at the heart of our world, of a dynamism of communion (love, forgiveness, reconciliation) incarnate in the existence of a community (the Church) where that love-reconciliation is lived out day by day. This great sign fosters in addition other manifestations of the new life in Christ which reveal different facets of the 'multicoloured grace of God' (1 Pet 4.10).

Among these signs, an important place must be accorded to *freedom*. Already in the Hebrew Scriptures, God is revealed as the Liberator, the One who creates a people — a historical subject — by breaking the bonds that kept it captive. The New Testament takes up this vision and discloses its roots in the human heart. By the unmerited gift of his love, God opens up a space of freedom where human beings can be truly themselves, since love is at the opposite extreme from constraint. Love engenders life rather than restraining or stifling it, by creating a context of trust and acceptance where people are stimulated to develop all their latent possibilities.

'Christ freed us so that we might be free', writes St Paul, and he continues, 'You were called to freedom'

(Gal 5.1, 13). He places this gift/call in a direct relationship with the Holy Spirit: 'where the Spirit of the Lord is, there is freedom' (2 Cor 3.17b). For Paul, the source of this freedom is the new relationship with God that comes through faith expressed in baptism. In Christ, the Son, we ourselves become God's sons and daughters: 'God sent into our hearts the Spirit of his Son, who calls out: Abba, Father!' (Gal 4.6; cf. Rom 8.15–16). Calling God 'Abba' means expressing an attitude of complete trust; it means leaving behind all forms of fear and submission characteristic of slavery (Gal 4.7; Rom 8.15a; 1 John 4.18).

This attitude of confident, almost carefree freedom often receives the name *parrhēsia* in the New Testament. In classical Greek, the word *parrhēsia* referred to the freedom of speech which was the inalienable right of citizens of the Greek city-states. St Luke employs the expression in the Acts of the Apostles to describe the assurance with which the first Christians proclaimed the Good News of salvation (Acts 4.13, 29, 31 etc.). Elsewhere, the word means above all the fact that believers can approach God without fear or shame, knowing that this is the Abba who loves them (1 John 2.28; 3.21; 4.17; 5.14; Heb 4.16; 10.19; Eph 3.12).

Things become more complicated when we attempt to explain how this freedom, born of the new relationship with God, is lived out in daily life. It is true that those who enter into the new covenant are liberated, by God's forgiveness (cf. Jer 31.34b), from the consequences of an inauthentic way of life (Rom 6.14; 8.2; John 8.34–36). They are likewise freed from the irksome necessity of following an outward

Law (Gal 5.18) because they benefit from the presence of that 'inward Law' which is the Spirit (Jer 31.33; Ezek 36.27) and which St James calls 'a Law of freedom' (James 1.25; 2.12). But this 'freedom-from' is incomplete unless it is accompanied by a 'freedom-for'.

In other words, in our existence on this earth, freedom does not exist either in a pure state or as a static reality. Every way of life has consequences that either widen or narrow the field of our freedom. That is why St Paul writes to the Galatians 'Christ freed us so that we might remain free. So stand firm and do not place yourselves again under the yoke of slavery' (Gal 5.1). In other words, 'Since the Spirit is the source of our life, we should likewise follow the Spirit's promptings' (Gal 5.25). This means 'walking in the Spirit' (Gal 5.16), in other words choosing to live a life that corresponds to the presence of God's Spirit in us. This kind of life produces what Paul calls 'the fruit of the Spirit', a single multi-faceted reality made up of charity, joy, peace, patience and so on. Diametrically opposed to this are 'the works of the flesh', which are characterized by discord and destructiveness (Gal 5.13–26). These lead only to spiritual death, whereas the Spirit in us is a source of life and peace (Rom 8.5–13).

Christian liberty thus has nothing in common with a devil-may-care attitude or with a lack of clear direction. It comes to full flowering in those who freely choose to serve others out of love (Gal 5.13; 1 Cor 9.19; 1 Pet 2.16). Freedom is not anarchy: life together requires a certain harmony (1 Cor 14.26–40) so that each person can find the room for personal growth. In short, like all the Christian values, freedom is not individualistic: its source and goal are found in communion.

Questions for Reflection

1. What aspects of contemporary society restrict our freedom? How does the Gospel help us to achieve that freedom which is not an absence of conditioning but means freely consenting, out of love, to follow the way of the Lord?

2. To what extent does the biblical and Christian understanding of freedom correct and complete the way we spontaneously view freedom?

3. What can we do to create, in our communities (family, parish, neighbourhood, etc.), a climate that allows true freedom to develop? Is there a contradiction between freedom and responsibility?

V

CREATIVE DISCONTENT

THE ATTITUDE of *parrhēsia*, the confident assurance that is an expression of Christian freedom, is sometimes linked to another important dimension of the new life in Christ. The letter to the Hebrews speaks of 'the *parrhēsia* of hope' (Heb 3.6; cf. 2 Cor 3.12; Phil 1.20). From the beginning, the openness to a coming fulfilment that we call hope is a fundamental characteristic of the biblical message. This hope is rooted in God's faithfulness: since God is faithful, believers can always, after each period of forgetfulness, begin their journey once again in God's company. In the darkest moments of Israel's history, the prophets proclaimed their conviction that beyond the difficulties of the present, God was preparing a new and brighter future for the nation.

In 'the Torah and the Prophets', hope is linked to the notion of *promise*, a notion found in the Hebrew Scriptures from beginning to end. 'I will make you a great nation', God had told Abraham (Gen 12.2), and throughout the history recounted in the Bible this promise of greater life constantly reappears in a great variety of guises. For the followers of Jesus Christ, however, this many-sided promise has finally been fulfilled: Paul says that 'all God's promises have their "yes" in him' (2 Cor 1.20). It is thus logical to ask whether, strictly speaking, in the new covenant hope has not lost its reason for being.

The answer to this question is of the utmost significance for our understanding of the Bible. With the coming of Christ and the definitive gift of the Holy Spirit, hope does not disappear but instead changes its character. It becomes stronger, more certain and, at the same time, its centre of gravity shifts from the future to the present. In this way, it reveals its divine character and appears more to human eyes as a paradoxical reality.

A verse from the letter to the Romans is fundamental in this regard:

And our hope does not disappoint us, because the love of God has been poured into our hearts through the Holy Spirit who has been given to us.

(Rom 5.5)

This text explains just how Christian hope is different from all other forms of what people call hope. Human hopes are simple wishes for the future, expressions of our desire that may be very noble, but are nevertheless without any real existence or guarantee that they will in fact become reality. The hope Paul speaks about, however, is already, so to speak, a present reality. It is the presence of God's love in person, the Holy Spirit, alive and active within us.

We thus reach the surprising conclusion that the gift of the Spirit, the object of the promise, is at the same time a source of hope. In other words, God's love is so dynamic that it has the paradoxical effect of quenching our thirst while at the same time awakening an even greater one. Fulfilment is shown to be not so much a static state of fruition as a source of creative discontent.* Thus the new covenant is not only new with respect to the old; it is new with respect to itself, because it involves a constant process of renewal that is known as hope.

The blessing at the end of the letter to the Romans emphasizes strongly this link between the Spirit and hope:

May the God of hope fill you with all joy and peace in believing, so that you may overflow with hope by the power of the Holy Spirit.

(Rom 15.13)

We have discovered a fundamental difference between the hope that comes from God and our ordinary human hopes. But now, a final reconciliation takes place. We witness another apparent paradox: the 'overflowing' of God's hope in us brings us into solidarity with the world that is still far from

---

*'[God] both satisfies your hunger, and does not. What I say is surprising. If I were to say that he satisfies you, I fear that, feeling that you are full, you would wish to get up and leave, as after dinner or after supper. So what shall I say? That he does not satisfy you? Then I fear that you would appear to be needy, and you would consider yourself more deprived, as if you were lacking something that should fill you. What shall I say, then, except what can be said, something that can scarcely be imagined? That he both satisfies you, and does not satisfy you, because I find both in Scripture. For it says: *Happy those who are hungry, for they will be filled* (Luke 6.21), and again, speaking of Wisdom: *Whoever eats you will be hungry again; and whoever drinks you will be thirsty again* (Sirach 24.21). Or rather, it says not 'again' but 'still' (. . .) What does that mean — to be thirsty while still drinking? Never to get tired' (St Augustine, *On Psalm LXXXV*, 24).

God, with all the human longings that in themselves are a sign of suffering, of not-yet-possessing. Speaking of all the yearning and the suffering of creation, St Paul compares it to the pangs of childbirth (Rom 8.18–22), since Christ's resurrection assures us of a final victory. But, continues the apostle, 'we too, who possess the first-fruits of the Spirit, groan inwardly ...' (Rom 8.23). The presence of the Spirit in us does not give us a privileged status apart from the world; it brings us more deeply into solidarity with the longing and suffering of creation; we join in its 'groaning'. And yet at the same time we live in hope, aware that, in Christ, the new creation is already a reality, that 'the darkness is being scattered and the true light is already shining' (1 John 2.8).

In the above verse of the letter to the Romans, to describe the presence of the Spirit in us, St Paul uses the word 'first-fruits'. Elsewhere he will call it a 'pledge', 'guarantee' or 'down payment' (2 Cor 1.22; 5.5; Eph 1.14), or a 'seal' (Eph 1.13; 4.30). All these expressions, which refer to a form of presence that is certain but incomplete, can perhaps be understood best in connection with the gospel image of the seed (e.g. Mark 4.8, 26–32). The foundation of Christian hope is the already active presence in us of God's Creator Spirit, an extremely dynamic reality that will never cease bearing fruit, a source of Newness that renews everything it touches.

Questions for Reflection

1. How does the modern belief in a continuous and irreversible progress help (or hinder) our understanding of hope in the Bible?

2. In the history of the people of the Bible, God's promise is attached to realities of this world (posterity, a land, an era of peace . . .) while at the same time going beyond them. In our lives, what does it mean to possess a hope fully incarnated in the realities around us but which always looks beyond them, towards a goal that is neither absorbed by the concerns of daily life nor a running away from them?

3. What is the role of believers in a situation threatened by despair, where the road to the future seems blocked? In a society marked by self-contentment and affluence?

VI

A PARADOXICAL JOY

THE NEW life in Christ in no way places us in a privileged situation, on a peaceful mountain-top far removed from the pain and struggles of the world below. On the contrary, the gift of hope already active in us brings us into a deep solidarity with the world that considers or wishes itself to be far from God: we should not forget that the first thing Jesus did after his baptism was to follow the prompting of the Holy Spirit and go out into the wilderness (Mark 1.12).

But if the Spirit impels us, in the steps of Christ, to be witnesses to Light where the darkness of evil is dominant, that also implies that we are given the courage and the strength necessary for this task. 'God is faithful, and will not let you be tried beyond your abilities. With the trial he will also provide the way out and the ability to bear it' (1 Cor 10.13). That is the principal meaning of the word 'Paraclete', used by Jesus to speak of the Holy Spirit (John 14.16, 26; 15.26; 16.7): a defender, a trustworthy support amidst the tribulations of an indifferent or hostile world.

Speaking to his disciples about the persecution they will have to undergo, Jesus tells them, 'Don't be anxious about what you will say ... It will not be you speaking, but the Holy Spirit' (Mark 13.11). Jesus knows well that, in this world, the life of resurrection will sometimes take the form of the cross. There have always been, of course, Christians who suffer an active persecution, and this is still true today; but most of us will usually experience something more subtle — the disdain, or perhaps merely the indifference, accorded to someone who openly witnesses to Christ and his Gospel.

But there is one text in the New Testament that even goes further. It tells us that 'all those who wish to live with fervour in Christ Jesus will be persecuted' (2 Tim 3.12). How can such a global statement be understood? Most of the time, it means we will experience an 'inner persecution'. Whether we like it or not, we are all marked by a society whose priorities are not those of the Gospel, and this means that being faithful to Christ will often involve an inner struggle. In such times of inner combat that can even bring us to the point of doubt, we can rely on Christ's promise when he assures us that, in times of trial, his Spirit is with us in an even more tangible way.

In the Hebrew Bible, the word that most clearly evokes the fulfilment of all God's promises is the word *shalom*, generally translated as 'peace' but possessing richer overtones — happiness, well-being, security, fulfilment and so on:

I will make with them a covenant of peace and banish wild animals from the land, so that they may live in the wild and sleep in the woods securely ... I will send down the showers in their season; they shall be showers of blessing. The trees of the field shall yield their fruit, and the earth shall yield its increase. They shall be secure on their soil ... I will break the bars of their yoke, and save them from the hands of those who enslaved them ... They shall no more be consumed with hunger in the land, and no longer suffer the insults of the nations.

(Ezek 34.25–29)

Experiencing this peace gives birth to *joy*, an inner state where all the hidden wellsprings of a person are liberated, where an inner vitality springs up and overflows at the sight of the marvels God is accomplishing:

> Sing aloud, O daughter Zion;
> shout for joy, O Israel!
> Rejoice and exult with all your heart,
> O daughter Jerusalem!
> The Lord has taken away the judgments against you,
> he has turned away your enemies.
> The king of Israel, the Lord, is in your midst;
> you shall fear disaster no more ...
> The Lord, your God, is in your midst
> a warrior who gives victory;
> he will rejoice over you with gladness,
> he will renew you in his love;
> he will exult over you with loud singing
> as on a day of festival.

(Zeph 3.14–18a)

It may seem paradoxical that, in the New Testament, this peace and joy, fruits of the resurrection (John 20.19–21), are most often found in a context of suffering and persecution. They are present especially where there are resistances to the spread of God's new life among human beings.

In John's gospel, the source of peace is the presence of the Spirit who sustains us in the difficulties that are an inevitable part of the pilgrimage of faith (John 14.26–27). This peace enables us to remain faithful and joyful in the midst of the turbulence of society:

I have said these things to you so that in me you may have peace. In this world you will have troubles, but be confident: I have overcome the world!

(John 16.33)

In the same way, when Paul speaks of joy, he often refers in the same breath to his sufferings for the cause of the Gospel:

I am overflowing with joy in all our tribulations . . . I rejoice in the sufferings I endure for you . . . And you have become imitators of us and of the Lord, welcoming the Gospel message in the midst of trials, with joy from the Holy Spirit.

(2 Cor 7.4; Col 1.24; 1 Thess 1.6; cf. 1 Pet 4.13)

What is the meaning of this connection? It is one more proof of the centrality of the paschal mystery in the Christian life. Christian peace and joy are *paschal*, that is to say they are born in the darkest hour of the night; they are always a victory wrenched from 'the jaws of the lion' (cf. 2 Tim 4.17). For the disciple of Christ, the relationship between the cross and the resurrection is not primarily a chronological one. Historically speaking, of course, the resurrection follows the cross. But in a deep sense the cross of Christ casts its shadow over the whole of human history, and it is precisely when we are able to discern, in the meaninglessness of suffering, the figure of the cross, in other words the features of the God of love, that the miracle of the resurrection takes place once again. At such a moment we experience 'God's peace, which is beyond all understanding' (Phil 4.7) and 'a

joy beyond words and radiant with God's glory'
(1 Pet 1.8).

Questions for Reflection

1. What aspects of our society make it hard to be faithful to Christ? How can we draw from our relationship with God the serene strength necessary to persevere?
2. Have there been times when I discovered, in the midst of difficulties, the tangible presence of the Holy Spirit that brought me joy and peace?
3. What does the beginning of St John's first letter (1 John 1.1–4) teach us about the relationship between joy and fellowship or communion?

VII

THE SONG OF THE REDEEMED

FINALLY, THE last great sign of the new creation in the process of coming to birth is the *new song* that arises from its depths. The mark of hearts transformed by the Spirit of God is the trust-filled prayer, and above all the prayer of praise, that expresses already here on earth the fullness of a communion.

We do not always feel capable of such a prayer, which seems far beyond our human capabilities. St Paul had already understood that 'we do not know how to pray as we ought' (Rom 8.26). But then he added:

but the Spirit himself intercedes for us with groans too deep for words, and the One who searches hearts knows what the Spirit intends, because the Spirit intercedes for God's holy people according to the mind of God.

(Rom 8.26–27)

For a believer, then, prayer is an openness, or rather a surrender, to the Spirit's prayer in us. The Spirit prays in our place, and knows better than we do what is in us and what God wishes for us. This prayer within us is likewise the prayer of Christ, summed up in the word 'Abba' (Rom 8.15; Gal 4.6), the expression of childlike confidence, of an unconditional trust. It is no accident if, when the disciples ask to enter into Christ's own way of praying, he teaches them a prayer that begins with the words 'Our Father ... ' (Luke 11.1–4; Matt 6.9–13).

The gospel-writers report another prayer of Jesus' where we catch a kind of behind-the-scenes glimpse of the new creation in action. In Luke's gospel, it comes when the disciples return 'with joy' after Jesus has sent them out to spread throughout the land the Good News of God's Reign:

At that very moment, [Jesus] exulted in the Holy Spirit and said, 'I praise you, Father, Lord of heaven and earth, because you hid these things from the wise and learned, and revealed them to little ones. Yes, Father, that is what you willed in your goodness.'

(Luke 10.21)

Here we have a definitive expression of the new song motivated by the awareness of God's activity which is renewing the universe. The sign of this renewal is an overturning of the values of a civilization founded on human power and self-justification; it is therefore expressed in the importance given to 'little ones'. Those who take the Gospel message to heart are, in the eyes of this civilization, doomed to disappear, beings who are insignificant, of little worth. And yet with and through them, God is in the process of creating a new world.

And among these 'little ones' is found, first and foremost, Jesus himself. For that reason, all who join in his new song become able through him to glimpse the very depths of the mystery of God:

'All things have been entrusted to me by my Father, and no one knows who the Son is but the Father, and no one knows who the Father is but the Son and the one to whom the Son wishes to reveal him.'

(Luke 10.22)

The disciples are granted the possibility of being present at the definitive turning-point of history, of seeing and hearing something absolutely new (Luke 10.23–24; Matt 13.35). But this newness did not simply mark one particular moment of history; since the resurrection of Christ it has been lying hidden under the surface of the old world, always ready to spring up once again.

The Revelation of St John, perhaps the most enigmatic of all the biblical books, indicates most clearly this permanent presence of the ongoing new creation across the ages. The book is framed by two visions: on the one hand the Risen Christ who comes on the clouds of heaven to take possession of his Kingdom (Rev 1.5–7), and on the other the Holy City, the new Jerusalem, coming down from heaven to be the dwelling-place of human beings in a renewed universe (Rev 21.1–4). All of human history, with its immense load of trials and misfortunes, plays itself out, like a great cosmic liturgy, within this victory already achieved, the victory of a love stronger than death. Thus the faithful can already sing a 'new song' (Rev 5.9; 14.3), and their song is clear proof that 'the former things have gone away', consumed in the transfiguring fire of the One who makes all things new (Rev 21.4–5).

Questions for Reflection

1. The book of Daniel contains a tale of three young men praising the Lord in a fiery furnace (Dan 3). In what way is this a good image of Christian prayer?

2. Is the prayer of our local Christian communities a true expression of the new life that is in us? What can we do to give it new vitality?

3. How does the end of Luke's gospel (Luke 24.50–53) express the essential aspects of the new covenant?

THE TAIZÉ COMMUNITY

IN FOUNDING the Taizé Community, Brother Roger has attempted to open up ways of healing the divisions between Christians and — through reconciliation of Christians — to overcome certain conflicts within the human family.

When he arrived alone in the village of Taizé in August 1940, at the age of 25, he was preparing to create a community where reconciliation could become a concrete reality every day. He wanted to accomplish this at the heart of the distress of the time, in the midst of World War II. He began by giving shelter to refugees, notably Jews.

For two years, Taizé's founder remained alone, then gradually he was joined by other brothers. In 1949, they made a lifetime commitment to common life and to celibacy. At the beginning, the brothers came from different Protestant backgrounds, but Catholic brothers soon joined the community, which today includes brothers from over twenty different countries. Some live in small groups, sharing the conditions of poor neighbourhoods in Asia, Africa, South and North America. From 1962 onwards, with great discretion, brothers and young people sent by Taizé were constantly visiting the countries of Eastern Europe, to be close to those who were trapped within their own frontiers.

The brothers accept neither gifts nor donations, not even their own personal inheritances. They earn their living and share with others solely by their work.

Taizé and the young

From 1957–58 onwards, young people have been coming to Taizé in ever greater numbers. From Portugal or India, from Russia or Kenya, they take part week after week in meetings bringing together young adults from 35 to 70 nations. Some weeks, there are as many as 6,000. Three times a day, everyone gathers for prayer in the Church of Reconciliation (built in 1962, enlarged in 1990–91).

Hundreds of thousands of young people have thus spent time on the hill of Taizé. They are looking for a meaning for their life at the wellsprings of faith: they are preparing themselves to take on responsibilities in the places where they live.

Since 1966, the Sisters of St Andrew, a Catholic community founded 750 years ago, have been living in a nearby village and are responsible for part of the welcoming of visitors.

A pilgrimage of trust on earth

To support the young in their commitments, Taizé started a 'pilgrimage of trust on earth'. This pilgrimage does not organize young people into a movement around the community but invites them to be creators of peace and reconciliation in their towns and villages, in their local Church, with all the generations, from little children to the elderly. As a stage in the pilgrimage, at the end of every year a six-day-long European meeting brings together many thousands of young adults in one of the major cities of Eastern or Western Europe. Similar meetings also take place in Asia, America and Africa. The year's end meeting is an occasion for Brother Roger to address an open letter to the young. Translated into 60 languages, the letter serves as a basis for reflection throughout the following year.

Address: The Taizé Community, 71250 Taizé, France. Tel: (33) 85.50.30.30; welcome (33) 85.50.30.02. Fax: (33) 85.50.30.15. E-mail: taize@cpe.ipl.fr

OTHER BOOKS FROM TAIZÉ

THE TAIZÉ EXPERIENCE
A book of photographs by Vladimir Sichov with texts by Brother Roger.

THE STORY OF TAIZÉ
A detailed account of Taizé from the beginnings to the present-day intercontinental meetings. By J. L. González Balado.

NO GREATER LOVE: SOURCES OF TAIZÉ
By Brother Roger. Expresses the fundamental vocation of Taizé and includes the 'Little Source' of Taizé.

HIS LOVE IS A FIRE
A section from Brother Roger's writings over 25 years gathered into one volume.

Geoffrey Chapman Mowbray, Wellington House, 125 Strand, London WC2R 0BB, UK.
Geoffrey Chapman Mowbray, c/o Charles Paine Pty Ltd, 8 Ferris Street, North Paramatta, NSW 2151, Australia.
The Liturgical Press, St John's Abbey, Collegeville, MN 56321, USA.

SONGS AND PRAYERS FROM TAIZÉ
A wide range of suggestions for preparing prayers in groups and parishes, together with fifty songs from Taizé, each with its musical setting, in its original language and an English-language version for singing.

Geoffrey Chapman Mowbray.

Rainbow Book Agencies Pty Ltd, 241 St Georges Road, PO Box 58, Northcote, Vic. 3070, Australia.

GIA Publications, 7404 S. Mason Avenue, Chicago, IL 60638, USA.